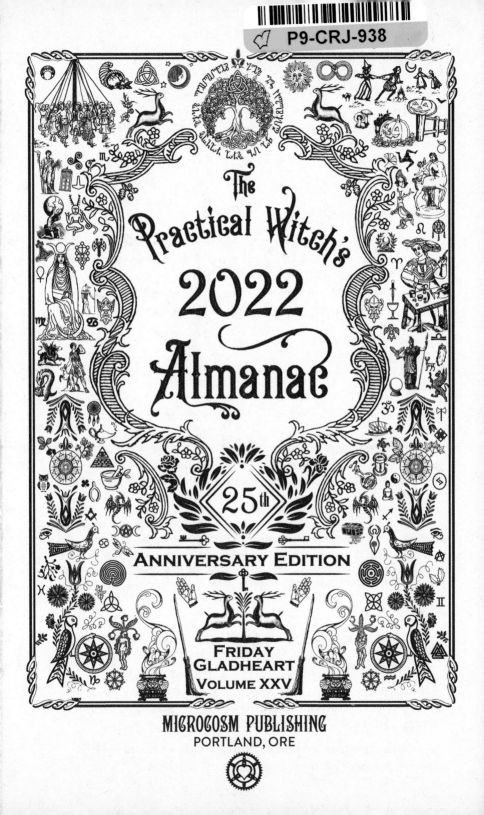

The Practical Witch's 2022 Almanac

25th ANNIVERSARY EDITION

FRIDAY GLADHEART

VOLUME XXV

MICROCOSM PUBLISHING

PORTLAND, ORE

PRACTICAL WITCH'S ALMANAC 2022:
25TH ANNIVERSARY EDITION

© 2021 Friday Gladheart
© This edition Microcosm Publishing 2021
First edition - 10,000 copies - November 10, 2021
ISBN 978-1-62106-268-4
This is Microcosm #670
Edited by Lydia Rogue
Address all inquiries to Almanac@PracticalWitch.com

To join the ranks of high-class stores that feature Microcosm titles, talk to your local rep: In the U.S. **COMO** (Atlantic), **FUJII** (Midwest), **BOOK TRAVELERS WEST** (Pacific), **TURNAROUND** (Europe), **UTP/MANDA** (Canada), **NEW SOUTH** (Australia/New Zealand), **GPS** in Asia, Africa, India, South America, and other countries, or **FAIRE** in the gift market.

For a catalog, write or visit:
Microcosm Publishing
2752 N Williams Ave.
Portland, OR 97227
https://microcosm.pub/PracticalWitch

The data in this almanac is calculated for Central Time with Daylight Savings Time already accounted for when it is active in most areas of the United States. In 2022, this is from March 13th to November 6th

Converting to any time zone in the world is simple with the map and table on pages 12-13.

MICROCOSM · PUBLISHING

MICROCOSM PUBLISHING is Portland's most diversified publishing house and distributor with a focus on the colorful, authentic, and empowering. Our books and zines have put your power in your hands since 1996, equipping readers to make positive changes in their lives and in the world around them. Microcosm emphasizes skill-building, showing hidden histories, and fostering creativity through challenging conventional publishing wisdom with books and bookettes about DIY skills, food, bicycling, gender, self-care, and social justice. What was once a distro and record label was started by Joe Biel in his bedroom and has become among the oldest independent publishing houses in Portland, OR. We are a politically moderate, centrist publisher in a world that has inched to the right for the past 80 years.

Global labor conditions are bad, and our roots in industrial Cleveland in the 70s and 80s made us appreciate the need to treat workers right. Therefore, our books are MADE IN THE USA.

Did you know that you can buy our books directly from us at sliding scale rates? Support a small, independent publisher and pay less than Amazon's price at **www.Microcosm.Pub**

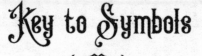

Key to Symbols

Moon Phases

● New Moon
◗ First Quarter
○ Full Moon
◖ Last/3rd Quarter

Sabbats

☸ Traditional Sabbats
⊕ Exact Cross-Quarters

Zodiac Symbols

The variety of symbols used to
represent astrological (Zodiac) signs

♈ ♈ Aries
♉ ♉ Taurus
♊ ♊ Gemini
♋ ♋ Cancer
♌ ♌ Leo
♍ ♍ Virgo

♎ ♎ Libra
♏ ♏ Scorpio
♐ ♐ Sagittarius
♑ ♑ Capricorn
♒ ♒ Aquarius
♓ ♓ Pisces

Celestial Symbols

☿ Mercury   ☼ Sun   ℞ Retrograde

→ Moon Enters Sign   ☼→ Sun Enters Sign

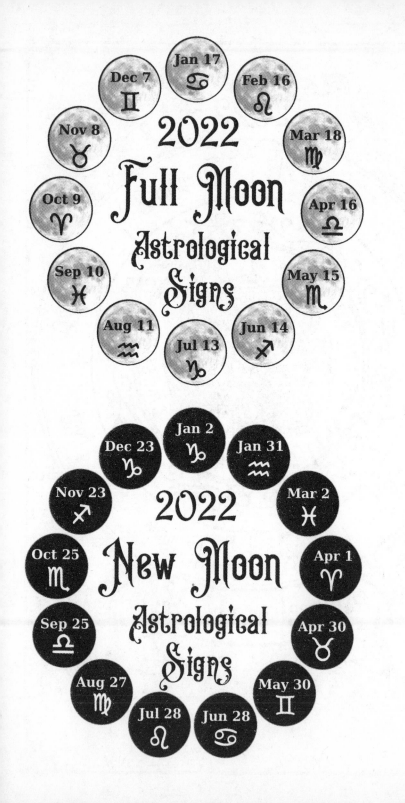

Merry Meet

The Practical Witch's Almanac is intended to be your daily guide to discovering the magic and beauty within you and throughout the natural world.

Beginners will find clear and practical guides, while advanced practitioners may discover new approaches to help rekindle their magic. Welcome, thank you for being here, and may your year be blessed.

Aloud we speak the names of the ancients,
Dancing spirals under bright moonlit skies,
We walk our paths with courage and joy;
We are healers, scholars, seekers, the wise.

WITCHACADEMY
— Founded in 1996 by Friday Gladheart —

TAROT HERBS WITCHCRAFT

WitchAcademy.org Annual Enrollment

Table of Contents

The Directories

January

Mo	Tu	We	Th	Fr	Sa	Su
					1	2
3	4	5	6	7	8	9
10	11	12	13	14	15	16
(17)	18	19	20	21	22	23
24	25	26	27	28	29	30
31						

2:● 9:◑ 17:○ 25:◐ 31:●

February

Mo	Tu	We	Th	Fr	Sa	Su
	1	✸	<u>3</u>	4	5	6
7	8	9	10	11	12	13
14	15	(16)	17	18	19	20
21	22	23	24	25	26	27
28						

2:✸ 8:◑ 16:○ 23:◐

May

Mo	Tu	We	Th	Fr	Sa	Su
						✸
2	3	4	<u>5</u>	6	7	8
9	10	11	12	13	14	(15)
16	17	18	19	20	21	22
23	24	25	26	27	28	29
30	31					

1:✸ 8:◐ 15:○ 22:◐ 30:●

June

Mo	Tu	We	Th	Fr	Sa	Su
		1	2	3	4	5
6	7	8	9	10	11	12
13	(14)	15	16	17	18	19
20	✸	22	23	24	25	26
27	28	29	30			

7:◑ 14:○ 20:◐ 21:✸ 28:●

September

Mo	Tu	We	Th	Fr	Sa	Su
			1	2	3	4
5	6	7	8	9	(10)	11
12	13	14	15	16	17	18
19	20	21	✸	23	24	25
26	27	28	29	30		

3:◐ 10:○ 17:◑ 22:✸ 25:●

October

Mo	Tu	We	Th	Fr	Sa	Su
					1	2
3	4	5	6	7	8	(9)
10	11	12	13	14	15	16
17	18	19	20	21	22	23
24	25	26	27	28	29	30
✸						

2:◐ 9:○ 17:◑ 25:● 31:✸

✸ Traditional Sabbat   <u>0</u> Exact Cross-Quarter

March

Mo	Tu	We	Th	Fr	Sa	Su
	1	2	3	4	5	6
7	8	9	10	11	12	13
14	15	16	17	(18)	19	✹
21	22	23	24	25	26	27
28	29	30	31			

2:● 10:◑ 18:○ 20:✹ 25:◐

April

Mo	Tu	We	Th	Fr	Sa	Su
				1	2	3
4	5	6	7	8	9	10
11	12	13	14	15	(16)	17
18	19	20	21	22	23	24
25	26	27	28	29	30	

1:● 9:◑ 16:○ 23:◐ 30:●

July

Mo	Tu	We	Th	Fr	Sa	Su
				1	2	3
4	5	6	7	8	9	10
11	12	(13)	14	15	16	17
18	19	20	21	22	23	24
25	26	27	28	29	30	31

6:◑ 13:○ 20:◐ 28:●

August

Mo	Tu	We	Th	Fr	Sa	Su
✹	2	3	4	5	6	7
8	9	10	(11)	12	13	14
15	16	17	18	19	20	21
22	23	24	25	26	27	28
29	30	31				

1:✹ 5:◑ 11:○ 18:◐ 27:●

November

Mo	Tu	We	Th	Fr	Sa	Su
	1	2	3	4	5	6
7	(8)	9	10	11	12	13
14	15	16	17	18	19	20
21	22	23	24	25	26	27
28	29	30				

1:◑ 8:○ 16:◐ 23:● 30:◑

December

Mo	Tu	We	Th	Fr	Sa	Su
			1	2	3	4
5	6	(7)	8	9	10	11
12	13	14	15	16	17	18
19	20	✹	22	23	24	25
26	27	28	29	30	31	

7:○ 16:◐ 21:✹ 23:● 29:◑

◑ 1st Quarter　○ Full　◐ Last Quarter　● New

Welcome to the 2022 Almanac

The Practical Witch's Almanac unites modern knowledge and science with traditional wisdom and Witchcraft. For the past two hundred years, almanacs have been embellished with elaborate woodcuts and engravings. Your almanac blends this classic styling with a magical flair.

Of course, no almanac would be complete without the odd bits of trivia, useful facts, recipes, and household tips. You'll find these sprinkled throughout your almanac, and all with a distinctively Practical Witch emphasis.

The Directories

Due to overwhelming demand from readers, the magical, metaphysical, and spiritual associations of plants[1], stones, tarot, etc. have returned. These correspondences have been expanded for this anniversary edition and include some notes from my book of shadows. These directories maintain the perennial value of your almanac beyond 2022.

Using Your Almanac

Living in harmony with nature's cycles is a great way to stay on track in reaching your goals. Your almanac's calendars, lunar planners, and weekly planner pages are just the tools needed to help.

Calendar Pages: At the beginning of each month, you'll find a calendar on the left side page. This calendar is handy for noting appointments, pet medication schedules, bills, etc. Sabbats, moon phases, and moon signs are marked on this calendar. When you need more detailed information just flip to the weekly planner pages. When a dates appears underlined and bold in the worksheets, it is a U.S. Federal Holiday.

---

1   Botanical correspondences include binomial (scientific) names for a few of the plants that are often misidentified.

The calendar page also gives you queues to help broaden your magical and spiritual studies. You can follow this schedule of study queues to delve deeper into a wide range of areas such as the tarot, runes, stones, plants, and a worldwide selection of deities.

Lunar Planners: On the page opposite each calendar and the study queues is your lunar planner. This is a list of the days of the month with the corresponding moon phase for each day. It is particularly helpful for working with the energy of moon phases. If you are not familiar with this, check out the article *Working With Moon Phases*. Dates of federal holidays are **<u>bold and underlined</u>** just as they are in the calendar, and dates of the full moons, new moons, 1st quarters, and 3rd quarters appear in ***bold italics***.

Planner Pages: This is where your daily practice is focused. Each week begins on Monday (the moon's day). You will find detailed information about Sabbat times, astrological moon sign transits, meteor showers, exact times of moon phases, solstices and equinoxes, trivia, and historical information.

Bonus Features

You'll find a variety of free goodies to compliment your almanac at the official Practical-Witch.com website. **You can even sync the events in your almanac with any calendar app on your device.** Sign up for the weekly newsletter for updates about new great stuff. You can contact me directly through the website, and I welcome your feedback, corrections, reviews, rants, praise, questions, or just friendly hellos.

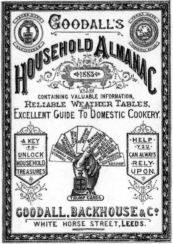

The 1883 Goodall's Household Almanac with its classic vintage styling.

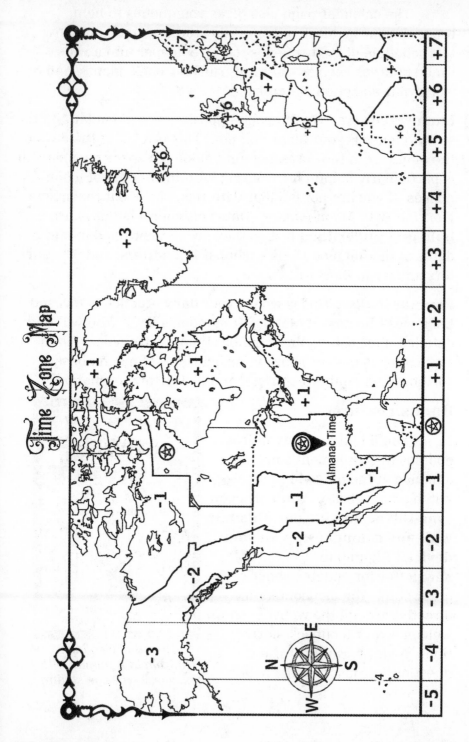

Time Zone Map

Time Zone Conversion Table

The planner pages are Central Time. Daylight Savings Time (DST) is accounted for when in effect. Add or subtract as indicated for your area.

Auckland, New Zealand +19	Amsterdam, Netherlands +7
New Plymouth, NZ +19	Madrid, Spain +7
Sydney, Australia +17	Rome, Italy +7
Melbourne, Australia +17	Dublin, Ireland +6
Cairns, Australia +16	Lisbon, Portugal +6
Adelaide, Australia +16.5	Prague, Czech Republic +6
Alice Springs, Australia +15.5	Reykjavik, Iceland +6
Tokyo, Japan +15	Glasgow, United Kingdom +6
Perth, Australia +14	Ittoqqortoormiit, Greenland +5
Shanghai, China +14	Nuuk, Greenland +3
Hong Kong, Hong Kong +14	Halifax, Canada +2
New Delhi, India +11.5	Bridgetown, Barbados +2
Moscow, Russia +9	Nassau, Bahamas +1
Cairo, Egypt +8	Ottawa, Canada +1
Athens, Greece +8	Port-au-Prince, Haiti +1
Rovaniemi, Finland +8	New York, NY, USA +1
Paris, France +7	Denver, CO, USA -1
Longyearbyen, Norway +7	Portland, OR, USA -2
Zürich, Switzerland +7	Phoenix, AZ, USA -1
Berlin, Germany +7	Honolulu, HI, USA -4

Hawaii, Puerto Rico, Guam, US Virgin Islands, and most of Arizona (except the Navajo Nation and parts of the north-east corner of the state) do not observe DST. For these or any areas without DST, subtract an hour (-1) from Almanac Time from March 13 to November 6.

January

National Blood Donor Month, National Braille Literacy Month, National Hobby Month, National Hot Tea Month. See tea recipes on pages 138.

Mon	Tue	Wed	Thu	Fri	Sat	Sun
					1 →♑	2 ●♑
3	4	5 →♒	6	7 →♈	8	9 ☽ →♒
10	11	12 →♊	13	14 ☿R	15 →♋	16
17 ○♋ →♌	18	19 ☀→♒	20 →♍	21	22 →♎	23
24 →♏	25 ☽	26	27 →♐	28	29 →♑	30
31 →♒ ●♒						

Study Queues: **Runes**-Fehu, Uruz **Tarot**-Fool, Magician, the four Aces **Botanicals**-Sage, Frankincense, Ginger, Chives, Wormwood **Stones**-Aventurine, Quartz Crystal, Citrine, Unakite **Deities**-Freya, Tithonus, Yemaya, Bast, Dôn, Shiva, The Morrígan

January Lunar Planner

Day		Moon
Sat	**1**	●
Sun	*2*	●
Mon	3	●
Tue	4	●
Wed	5	●
Thu	6	◐
Fri	7	◐
Sat	8	◐
Sun	*9*	◐
Mon	10	◐
Tue	11	◐
Wed	12	◐
Thu	13	○
Fri	14	○
Sat	15	○
Sun	16	○
Mon	**17**	○
Tue	18	○
Wed	19	○
Thu	20	○
Fri	21	○
Sat	22	○
Sun	23	○
Mon	24	◑
Tue	25	◑
Wed	26	◑
Thu	27	◑
Fri	28	◑
Sat	29	●
Sun	30	●
Mon 31		●

Monday, December 27, 2021

Moon is in Libra

Tuesday 28

National Card Playing Day
Moon enters Scorpio 3:17 pm

Wednesday 29

Pepper Pot Day

Thursday 30

Moon enters Sagittarius 5:08 pm

Friday 31

New Years Day (U.S. Federal Holiday observed)

Saturday, January 1, 2022

New Years Day
Sir James George Frazer Born
Moon enters Capricorn 5:02 pm

Sunday 2

● New Moon in Capricorn (Supermoon)

Monday, 3

Festival of Sleep Day
Moon enters Aquarius 4:44 pm
Quadrantids Meteor Shower

Tuesday 4

Trivia Day
Quadrantids Meteor Shower

Wednesday 5

Whip Cream Day
Moon enters Pisces 6:16 pm

Thursday 6

Bean Day

Friday 7

Programmers Day
Moon enters Aries 11:26 pm
Galileo discovers four of Jupiter's moons in 1610

Saturday 8

Bubble Bath Day
Venus will pass between us and the Sun,
      coming closest to Earth in its orbit

Sunday 9

◑ First Quarter 12:11 pm

Monday, 10

Peculiar People Day
Coming of Age Day (Japan)
Moon enters Taurus 8:47 am

Tuesday 11

Wednesday 12

Hot Tea Day (see page 138 for recipes)
Moon enters Gemini 9:08 pm

Thursday 13

Friday 14

☿℞ Mercury Retrograde

Saturday 15

National Hat Day
Moon enters Cancer 10:10 am

Sunday 16

Appreciate a Dragon Day

Monday, 17

Martin Luther King Jr. Day (U.S. Federal)
○ Full Moon in Cancer 5:48 pm
Moon enters Leo 10:03 pm

Tuesday 18

Wednesday 19

Sun enters Aquarius 8:39 pm

Thursday 20

Moon enters Virgo 8:02 am

Friday 21

National Granola Bar Day
National Hot Chocolate Day

Saturday 22

Moon enters Libra 4:02 pm

Sunday 23

Monday, 24

Compliment Day
Moon enters Scorpio 9:57 pm

Tuesday 25

Opposite Day
◑ Last Quarter 7:40 am

Wednesday 26

Australia Day

Thursday 27

Moon enters Sagittarius 1:34 am
National Chocolate Cake day

Friday 28

Saturday 29

National Seed Swap Day
Moon enters Capricorn 3:09 am

Sunday 30

Little Life Hacks

- Do your crystal and stone spheres roll around your altar? Stop the roll by tucking an elastic hair band under your altar cloth. No altar cloth? No problem! Look for napkin rings at antique and thrift stores. They come in a wide variety of designs and materials.

- Use dry-erase markers on appliances like the dish washer to leave notes for roommates or to mark items as clean or dirty.

- Hiding eggs for Ostara? Looking for unique party favors? Write fortunes or blessings on small pieces of paper. Roll the paper tightly into a tube and insert into the shell of a blown egg.

- T-molding can be found at lumber and home stores. Cut strips and attach them under counters to hold wine glasses, coffee pods, or wide-lidded spice jars.

- Paint protective symbols on walls in the same color as your wall paint, but with a different sheen. Most walls have a matte or eggshell finish, try painting your sigils and symbols with gloss or transparent glow-in-the-dark paint.

- Dying eggs for a spring Sabbat? Use a whisk to hold the eggs when dipping them into dye.

February

Black History Month (U.S.), LGBTQIA+ History Month (UK), American Heart Month, Great American Pie Month. This February is a black moon, see the article *Black & Blue Moons* for more information.

Mon	Tue	Wed	Thu	Fri	Sat	Sun
	1	2 ❋ →♏	3 ⊕ ☿Direct	4 →♈	5	6 →♉
7	8 ◑	9 →♊	10	11 →♋	12	13
14 →♌	15	16 ○♌ →♍	**17**	18 →♎ ☀→♏	19	20
21 →♏	22	23 ◑ →♐	24	25 →♑	26	27 →♒
28	Dates in the calendars and lunar planner pages display U.S. federal holidays in **<u>Bold/Underlined</u>** and primary moon phases are in ***Bold Italics***.					

Study Queues:
Runes-Thurisaz, Ansuz **Tarot-**High Priestess, Empress, the 4 twos
Botanicals-Rosemary, Cinnamon, Vervain, Catnip, Eucalyptus **Stones-**Rose Quartz, Garnet, Jasper, Rhodonite **Deities-**Phobetor, Brigit, Babalú Ayé, Mokosh, Loki, Persephone, Demeter, Proserpina, Ceres

February Lunar Planner

Tue	**1**	●
Wed	2	● �
Thu	3	● ⊕
Fri	4	◑
Sat	5	◑
Sun	6	◑
Mon	7	◗
Tue	*8*	◗
Wed	9	◗
Thu	10	◗
Fri	11	◗
Sat	12	◖
Sun	13	◖
Mon	14	○
Tue	15	○
Wed	*16*	○
Thu	**17**	○
Fri	18	○
Sat	19	○
Sun	20	○
Mon	**21**	◐
Tue	22	◐
Wed	**23**	◐
Thu	24	◑
Fri	25	◑
Sat	26	●
Sun	27	●
Mon	28	●

Monday, 31

Moon enters Aquarius 3:42 am
● New Moon in Aquarius 11:46 pm

Tuesday, February 1

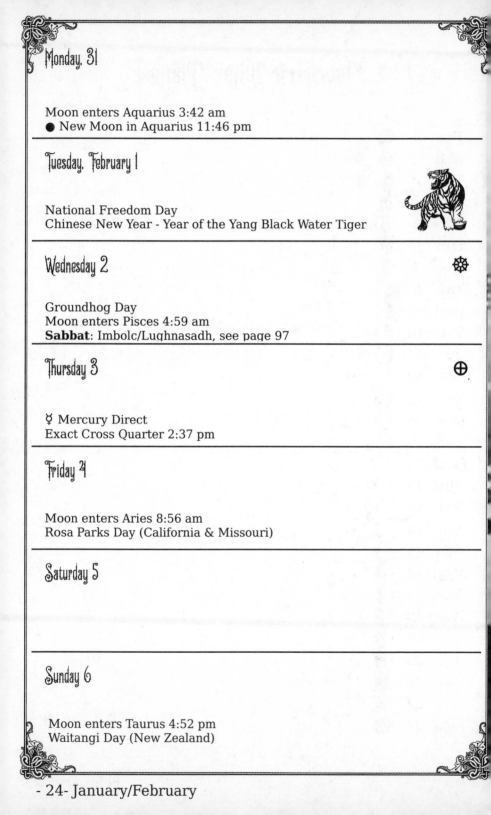

National Freedom Day
Chinese New Year - Year of the Yang Black Water Tiger

Wednesday 2

Groundhog Day
Moon enters Pisces 4:59 am
Sabbat: Imbolc/Lughnasadh, see page 97

Thursday 3

☿ Mercury Direct
Exact Cross Quarter 2:37 pm

Friday 4

Moon enters Aries 8:56 am
Rosa Parks Day (California & Missouri)

Saturday 5

Sunday 6

Moon enters Taurus 4:52 pm
Waitangi Day (New Zealand)

Monday, 7

Waitangi Day observed (New Zealand)

Tuesday 8

◗ First Quarter 7:50 am
National Kite Flying Day

Wednesday 9

Moon enters Gemini 4:27 am
National Pizza Day

Thursday 10

Friday 11

Moon enters Cancer 5:26 pm
National Foundation Day (Japan)

Saturday 12

Sunday 13

Monday, 14

Moon enters Leo 5:17 am
Valentine's Day

Tuesday 15

Lantern Festival
Susan B. Anthony Born

Wednesday 16

○ Full Moon in Leo 10:56 am
Moon enters Virgo 2:42 pm

Thursday 17

Friday 18

Sun enters Pisces 10:43 am
Moon enters Libra 9:51 pm

Saturday 19

Sunday 20

World Day of Social Justice

Monday, 21

Barbara Jordan Born
Moon enters Scorpio 3:19 am
Presidents Day (U.S. Federal)

Tuesday 22

Sybil Leek Born

Wednesday 23

Emperors Birthday (Japan)
◑ Last Quarter 4:32 pm
Moon enters Sagittarius 7:29 am
National Dog Biscuit Day

Thursday 24

National Chili Day

Friday 25

Moon enters Capricorn 10:27 am
Carnival (Brazil)

Saturday 26

Sunday 27

National Retro Day
Moon enters Aquarius 12:35 pm

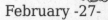

March

Craft Month, Irish American Heritage Month, Women's History Month, Social Workers Month

Mon	Tue	Wed	Thu	Fri	Sat	Sun
	1 →♋	2 ●♋	3 →♈	4	5	6 →♉
7	8 →♊	9	10 ◐	11 →♋	12	13 →♌
14	15 →♍	16	17	18 ○♍ →♎	19	20 ❋ →♏ ☀→♈
21	22 →♐	23	24 →♑	25 ◑	26 →♒	27
28 →♋	29	30	31 →♈			

Study Queues:
Runes-Raidho, Kenaz **Tarot**-Emperor, Hierophant, the 4 threes
Botanicals-Sandalwood, Dragon's Blood, Myrrh, Cloves, Jasmine **Stones**-Obsidian, Tourmaline, Labradorite, Malachite **Deities**-Odin, Iah, Sucellos, Baudihillie, Arianrhod, Guanyin

March Lunar Planner

Tue	1	
Wed	*2*	
Thu	3	
Fri	4	
Sat	5	
Sun	6	
Mon	7	
Tue	8	
Wed	9	
Thu	*10*	
Fri	11	
Sat	12	
Sun	13	
Mon	14	
Tue	15	
Wed	16	
Thu	17	
Fri	*18*	
Sat	19	
Sun	20	✾
Mon	21	
Tue	22	
Wed	23	
Thu	24	
Fri	*25*	
Sat	26	
Sun	27	
Mon	28	
Tue	29	
Wed	30	
Thu	31	

Monday, 28

Tuesday, March 1

Mardi Gras
Moon enters Pisces 2:53 pm
Zero Discrimination Day

Wednesday 2

Read Across America Day
● New Moon in Pisces 11:34 am

Thursday 3

World Wildlife Day
Moon enters Aries 6:52 pm
National Academy of Science founded in 1863

Friday 4

Employee Appreciation Day

Saturday 5

Sunday 6

Moon enters Taurus 2:00 am

Monday, 7

National Cereal Day

Tuesday 8

International Women's Day
Moon enters Gemini 12:39 pm

Wednesday 9

Thursday 10

◖ First Quarter 4:45 am
Harriet Tubman's Birthday

Friday 11

Douglas Adams's Birthday
Moon enters Cancer 1:24 am

Saturday 12

National Plant a Flower Day

Sunday 13

Moon enters Leo 2:31 pm
Daylight Saving Time begins 2:00am Set Clocks ahead +1 hour (U.S.)

Monday, 14

Pi Day
Albert Einstein Born
Day off for Benito Juárezs Birthday Memorial (Mexico)

Tuesday 15

Moon enters Virgo 11:59 am
Ides of March (Brutus stabs Caesar 44 B.C.E.)

Wednesday 16

Thursday 17

St. Patrick's Day
Roman Liberalia/Greek Bacchanalia

Friday 18

○ Full Moon in Virgo 2:17 am
Moon enters Libra 6:26 am
National Awkward Moments Day

Saturday 19

Sunday 20

International Day of Happiness
Equinox Sabbat 10:33 am
Moon enters Scorpio 10:44 am
Sun enters Aries 10:33 am

Monday, 21

World Poetry Day
International Day of Forests
World Day to Eliminate Racial Discrimination

Tuesday 22

World Water Day
Moon enters Sagittarius 1:59 pm

Wednesday 23

Puppy Day

Thursday 24

Moon enters Capricorn 4:54 pm
National Chocolate Covered Raisin Day

Friday 25

International Waffle Day
◑ Last Quarter 12:37 am

Saturday 26

Wear a Hat Day
Moon enters Aquarius 7:55 pm
Dr. Jonas Salk announces his polio vaccine

Sunday 27

Monday, 28

Moon enters Pisces 11:32 am
Weed Appreciation Day

Tuesday 29

National Vietnam War Veterans Day

Wednesday 30

Thursday 31

Moon enters Aries 4:30 am

Friday, April 1

April Fools Day
● New Moon in Aries 1:24 am

Saturday 2

Moon enters Taurus 11:50 am

Sunday 3

National Find a Rainbow Day

Birth Stones by the Month

Birth stones are also known as natal stones. The stones associated with each month have varied over the centuries and the most modern is listed first in the selections below.

Wearing the stone that corresponds with your birth month is said to help you think more clearly, keep your inner calm, and help you manifest your intentions more easily. From a practical perspective, they definitely encourage you to learn about stones and their properties!

January: Garnet
February: Amethyst, Pearl, Hyacinth (Zircon)
March: Bloodstone, Jasper, Aquamarine
April: Diamond, Sapphire, Quartz Crystal
May: Emerald, Agate, Chryoprase
June: Cat's Eye, Turquoise, Agate, Pearl,
      Moonstone, Alexandrite
July: Turquoise, Onyx, Ruby, Carnelian
August: Sardonyx, Carnelian, Moonstone,
      Topaz, Peridot, Spinel
September: Chrysolite, Sapphire, Lapis Lazuli
October: Opal, Aquamarine, Tourmaline
November: Topaz, Pearl, Citrine
December: Bloodstone, Ruby, Turquoise,
      Lapis Lazuli, Zircon, Tanzanite

Birth Stones by the Zodiac Sign

Aquarius: Garnet
Pisces: Amethyst
Aries: Bloodstone
Taurus: Sapphire
Gemini: Agate
Cancer: Emerald

Leo: Onyx
Virgo: Carnelian
Libra: Chrysolite
Scorpio: Beryl
Sagittarius: Topaz
Capricorn: Ruby

April

Child Abuse Prevention Month, Humor Month, Autism Awareness Month, Poetry Month, Volunteer Month, Sexual Assault Awareness Month. April 30th is a black moon. See page 106 for information about black moons.

Mon	Tue	Wed	Thu	Fri	Sat	Sun
				1 ●♈	2 →♉	3
4 →♊	5	6	7 →♋	8	9 ◐ →♌	10
11	12 →♍	13	14 →♎	15	16 ○♎ →♏	17
18 →♐	19 ☼→♉	20 →♑	21	22	23 ◑ →♒	24
25 →♓	26	27 →♈	28	29 →♉	30 ●♉	

Study Queues:
Runes-Gebo, Wunjo **Tarot**-Lovers, Chariot, the 4 fours **Botanicals**-Chamomile, Lemon Balm, Rose, Broom (Broomcorn) **Stones**-Amazonite, Celestite, Lapis Lazuli, Hematite, Numite **Deities**-Thor, Hermes, Andraste, Isis, Cáer, Zorya Utrennyaya, Zorya Vechernyaya, Zorya Polunochnaya

April Lunar Planner

Fri	*1*	🌑
Sat	2	🌑
Sun	3	🌑
Mon	4	🌑
Tue	5	🌒
Wed	6	🌒
Thu	7	🌒
Fri	8	🌒
Sat	*9*	🌓
Sun	10	🌓
Mon	11	🌓
Tue	12	🌔
Wed	13	🌔
Thu	14	🌔
Fri	15	🌕
Sat	*16*	🌕
Sun	17	🌕
Mon	18	🌖
Tue	19	🌖
Wed	20	🌖
Thu	21	🌖
Fri	22	🌗
Sat	*23*	🌗
Sun	24	🌗
Mon	25	🌘
Tue	26	🌘
Wed	27	🌘
Thu	28	🌑
Fri	29	🌑
Sat	*30*	🌑

Monday, 4

Maya Angelou Born
Moon enters Gemini 10:04 pm

Tuesday 5

Wednesday 6

National Tartan Day

Thursday 7

Moon enters Cancer 10:30 am
United Nations World Health Day

Friday 8

International Romani Day

Saturday 9

Moon enters Leo 10:59 pm
◐ First Quarter 1:47 am
National Name Yourself Day

Sunday 10

Monday, 11

National Pet Day

Tuesday 12

International Day of Human Space Flight
Moon enters Virgo 9:07 am
National Library Workers Day

Wednesday 13

```
        D₂
S₁ C₃ R₁ A₁ B₃ B₃ L₁ E₁
        Y₄
```

Thursday 14

Moon enters Libra 3:46 pm

Friday 15

Good Friday
U.S. Tax Day

Saturday 16

Mushroom Day
Margot Adler Born
Moon enters Scorpio 7:22 pm
○ Full Moon in Libra 1:55 pm

Sunday 17

Easter Sunday
National Haiku Poetry Day

Monday, 18

Moon enters Sagittarius

Tuesday 19

Bicycle Day
Sun enters Taurus 9:25 pm

Wednesday 20

 Four Twenty
Moon enters Capricorn 10:52 pm

Thursday 21

Tiradentes Day (Brazil)

Friday 22

Earth Day
Lyrids Meteor Shower
National Jelly Bean Day

Saturday 23

Lyrids Meteor Shower
◗ Last Quarter 6:56 am
Moon enters Aquarius 1:17 am
Order of the Garter Established

Sunday 24

Monday, 25

Moon enters Pisces 5:14 am
ANZAC Day (Australia & New Zealand)
National Telephone Day

Tuesday 26

National Pretzel Day

Wednesday 27

Administrative Professionals Day
National Tell a Story Day
Moon enters Aries 11:10 pm

Thursday 28

National Superhero Day
Take our Daughters and Sons to Work Day

Friday 29

Arbor Day
National Zipper Day
Shōwa Day (Japan)
Moon enters Taurus 7:19 pm

Saturday 30

International Jazz Day
● New Moon in Taurus 3:28 pm
Partial Solar Eclipse 1:45 pm

Sunday, May 1

❀

Lei Day (Hawaii)
Labour Day / May Day (Brazil & Mexico)
WitchAcademy.org Founded 1996
  Sabbat: Beltane/Samhain, see page 97

May

National Bike Month, Lupus Awareness Month, Foster Care Month, National Barbecue Month. May 15th is a total lunar eclipse.

Mon	Tue	Wed	Thu	Fri	Sat	Sun
						1 ☸
2 →♊	3	4 →♋	5 ⊕	6	7 →♌	8 ◐
9 →♍	10 ☿℞	11	12 →♎	13	14 →♏	15 ○♏
16 →♐	17	18 →♑	19	20 →♒ ☼→♊	21	22 ◑ →♓
23	24 →♈	25	26	27 →♉	28	29 →♊
<u>30</u> ●♊	31					

Study Queues:

Runes-Hagalaz, Naudhiz **Tarot**-Justice, Hermit, the 4 fives **Botanicals**-Bay, Thyme, Rue, Lavender, Hyssop, Poppy **Stones**-Cat's Eye, Tiger's Eye, Hawk's Eye, Moonstone **Deities**-Hel, Apollo, The Tuatha Dé Danann, Horus, Quetzalcoatl, Kannon

May Lunar Planner

Sun	1	🌑	✸
Mon	2	🌘	
Tue	3	🌘	
Wed	4	🌘	
Thu	5	🌘	⊕
Fri	6	🌗	
Sat	7	🌗	
Sun	*8*	🌗	
Mon	9	🌗	
Tue	10	🌖	
Wed	11	🌖	
Thu	12	🌕	
Fri	13	🌕	
Sat	14	🌕	
Sun	*15*	🌕	
Mon	16	🌕	
Tue	17	🌕	
Wed	18	🌕	
Thu	19	🌔	
Fri	20	🌔	
Sat	21	🌒	
Sun	*22*	🌒	
Mon	23	🌒	
Tue	24	🌒	
Wed	25	🌒	
Thu	26	🌑	
Fri	27	🌑	
Sat	28	🌑	
Sun	29	🌑	
__Mon 30__		🌑	
Tue	31	🌑	

Monday, 2

May Day (Ireland National Holiday)
Moon enters Gemini 5:46 am

Tuesday 3

Constitution Memorial Day (Japan)
World Press Freedom Day

Wednesday 4

Greenery Day (Japan)
May The Forth Be With You
Moon enters Cancer 6:05 pm

Thursday 5

⊕

Cinco de Mayo
Children's Day (Japan)
Exact Cross Quarter 7:25 am

Friday 6

Eta Aquarids Meteor Shower
National Nurses Day

Saturday 7

Eta Aquarids Meteor Shower
Herb Day, Kentucky DerbyMoon enters Leo 6:50 am
National Explosive Ordnance Disposal (EOD) Day

Sunday 8

Mothers Day
◗ First Quarter 7:21 pm

Monday, 9

Moon enters Virgo 5:53 pm

Tuesday 10

Christopher Penezak Born
☿R Mercury Retrograde

Wednesday 11

Thursday 12

International Nurses Day
Moon enters Libra 1:34 am

Friday 13

Saturday 14

Gabriel D. Fahrenheit Born
Moon enters Scorpio 5:34 am
World Migratory Bird Day

Sunday 15

Total Lunar Eclipse 8:32 pm
○ Full Moon in Scorpio 11:14 pm

Monday, 16

Honor Our LGBTQIA+ Elders Day
Moon enters Sagittarius 6:50 am

Tuesday 17

Wednesday 18

Moon enters Capricorn 7:02 am
Omar Khayyam Born

Thursday 19

Malcom X Born

Friday 20

National Bike to Work Day
Moon enters Aquarius 7:53 am
Sun enters Gemini 8:23 pm

Saturday 21

Armed Forces Day
Gwyddion Pendderwen Born
World Day of Cultural Diversity

Sunday 22

☽ Last Quarter 1:43 pm
Moon enters Pisces 10:49 am

Monday, 23

Victoria Day
National Lucky Penny Day

Tuesday 24

Moon enters Aries 4:39 pm
National Scavenger Hunt Day

Wednesday 25

Thursday 26

Friday 27

Moon enters Taurus 1:22 am
Morning Glory Zell-Ravenheart Born

Saturday 28

Sunday 29

Moon enters Gemini 12:22 pm

June

LGBTQIA+ Pride Month, Oceans Month, Adopt a Cat Month, Candy Month

Mon	Tue	Wed	Thu	Fri	Sat	Sun
		1 →♋	2	3 →♌ ☿Direct	4	5
6 →♍	7 ☽	8 →♎	9	10 →♏	11	12 →♐
13	14 ○♐ →♑	15	16 →♒	17	18 →♓	**19**
20 ☽ →♈	21 ✳ ☀→♋	22	23 →♉	24	25 →♊	26
27	28 →♋ ●♋	29	30 →♌			

Study Queues:
Runes-Isa, Jera **Tarot**-Wheel of Fortune, Strength, the 4 sixes
Botanicals-Basil, Yarrow, Mint, Mugwort, Violet, Narcissus **Stones**-
Amethyst, Zebra Stone, Aquamarine, Fluorite **Deities**-Ceridwen, Magni,
Set, Nuada, Áed, Clota

June Lunar Planner

Wed	1	●
Thu	2	●
Fri	3	●
Sat	4	●
Sun	5	●
Mon	6	●
Tue	*7*	◐
Wed	8	◐
Thu	9	◐
Fri	10	◐
Sat	11	○
Sun	12	○
Mon	13	○
Tue	*14*	○
Wed	15	○
Thu	16	○
Fri	17	○
Sat	18	○
Sun	**19**	◐
Mon	***20***	◐
Tue	21	◐ ❁
Wed	22	◐
Thu	23	◐
Fri	24	◐
Sat	25	●
Sun	26	●
Mon	27	●
Tue	*28*	●
Wed	29	●
Thu	30	●

Monday. 30

Joan of Arc Day
● New Moon in Gemini 5:30 am
Memorial Day (U.S. Federal)

Tuesday 31

Wednesday. June 1

National Go Barefoot Day
Moon enters Cancer 12:49 am

Thursday 2

Friday 3

☿ Mercury Direct
Moon enters Leo 1:38 pm
Marion Zimmer Bradley Born
National Repeat Day National Repeat Day

Saturday 4

Sunday 5

World Environment Day

Monday, 6

D Day
Moon enters Virgo 1:22 am
Queens Birthday (New Zealand)

Tuesday 7

British Museum Founded 1753
◑ First Quarter 9:48 am

Wednesday 8

National Best Friend Day
World Oceans Day
Moon enters Libra 10:22 am

Thursday 9

National Strawberry Rhubarb Pie Day

Friday 10

National Iced Tea Day
Moon enters Scorpio 3:41 pm

Saturday 11

Sunday 12

Anne Frank Born
Moon enters Sagittarius 5:31 pm

Monday, 13

Gerald Gardner Born

Tuesday 14

Flag Day
Moon enters Capricorn 5:14 pm
World Blood Donor Day
○ Full Moon in Sagittarius 6:51 am (Supermoon)

Wednesday 15

Nature Photography Day

Thursday 16

National Fudge Day
Moon enters Aquarius 4:44 pm

Friday 17

Starhawk Born

Saturday 18

National Go Fishing Day
Moon enters Pisces 6:01 pm

Sunday 19

Fathers Day
Juneteenth (U.S. Federal)

Monday, 20

American Eagle Day
World Refugee Day
Juneteenth Observed (U.S. Federal)
◖ Last Quarter 10:10 pm | Moon enters Aries 10:37 pm

Tuesday 21

❀

Solstice Sabbat 4:13 am
International Day of Yoga
Sun enters Cancer 4:13 am

Wednesday 22

Thursday 23

Moon enters Taurus 6:58 am

Friday 24

Janet Farrar Born
Take Your Dog to Work Day

Saturday 25

Day of the Seafarer
Moon enters Gemini 6:13 pm

Sunday 26

National Canoe Day

Monday, 27

Helen Keller Born

Tuesday 28

Scott Cunningham Born
Stewart Farrar Born
Moon enters Cancer 6:53 am
● New Moon in Cancer 9:52 pm

Wednesday 29

National Camera Day

Thursday 30

Moon enters Leo 7:39 pm
International Asteroid Day

Friday, July 1

Canada Day (Canadian National Holiday)
International Joke Day

Saturday 2

World UFO Day
Thurgood Marshall Born

Sunday 3

Compliment Your Mirror Day
Moon enters Virgo 7:31 am

Auspicious Days

Many almanacs include auspicious (favorable) days for fishing, planting, harvesting, cutting hair, etc. This is a very old tradition and below I've transcribed from The Grand Grimoire. Also known as The Red Dragon or Le Dragon Rouge, this grimoire was published c. 1704 (but claimed to be from the 1500s). The text accompanying this Table of Auspicious and Inauspicious Days provides some explanation,

"Many wise men believe this table was dictated to Abraham by an angel and that it determined his actions: he neither sowed nor transplanted except on auspicious days and for this reason everything went marvelously for him. If your ploughmen did likewise their yield would certainly increase."

Auspicious Days	Month	Inauspicious Days
3, 10, 27, 31	January	13, 23
7, 8, 18	February	2, 10, 17, 22
3, 9, 12, 14, 16	March	13, 19, 23, 28
5, 17	April	18, 20, 29, 30
1, 2, 4, 6, 9, 14	May	10, 17, 20
3, 5, 7, 9, 12, 23	June	4, 20
2, 6, 10, 23, 30	July	5, 13, 27
5, 7, 10, 14, 29	August	2, 13, 27, 31
6, 10, 13, 18, 30	September	13, 16, 18, 19
13, 16, 25, 31	October	3, 9, 27
1, 13, 23, 30	November	6, 25
10, 20, 29	December	15, 26, 31

July

National Ice Cream Month, National Cell Phone Courtesy Month

Mon	Tue	Wed	Thu	Fri	Sat	Sun
				1	2	3 →♍
4	5 →♎	6 ☽	7	8 →♏	9	10 →⚕
11	12 →♑	13 ○♑	14 →♒	15	16 →⚭	17
18 →♈	19	20 ☽ →♉	21	22 ☀→♌	23 →♊	24
25 →♋	26	27	28 →♌ ●♌	29	30 →♍	31

Study Queues:
Runes-Eihwaz, Pertho   **Tarot**-Hanged Man, Death, the 4 sevens
Botanicals-Basil, Yarrow, Mint, Mugwort, Violet, Narcissus   **Stones**-
Amethyst, Zebra Stone, Aquamarine, Fluorite   **Deities**-Ceridwen, Magni,
Set, Nuada, Áed, Clota

July Lunar Planner

Fri	1	
Sat	2	
Sun	3	
Mon	**4**	
Tue	5	
Wed	*6*	
Thu	7	
Fri	8	
Sat	9	
Sun	10	
Mon	11	
Tue	12	
Wed	*13*	
Thu	14	
Fri	15	
Sat	16	
Sun	17	
Mon	18	
Tue	19	
Wed	*20*	
Thu	21	
Fri	22	
Sat	23	
Sun	24	
Mon	25	
Tue	26	
Wed	27	
Thu	*28*	
Fri	29	
Sat	30	
Sun	31	

Monday, 4

Independence Day (U.S. Federal)

Tuesday 5

Moon enters Libra 5:25 pm

Wednesday 6

☽ First Quarter 9:14 pm
International Kissing Day

Thursday 7

World Chocolate Day
Global Forgiveness Day

Friday 8

Moon enters Scorpio 12:15 am

Saturday 9

Elias Howe Born 1819 (she invented the sewing machine)

Sunday 10

National Piña Colada Day
Moon enters Sagittarius 3:34 am

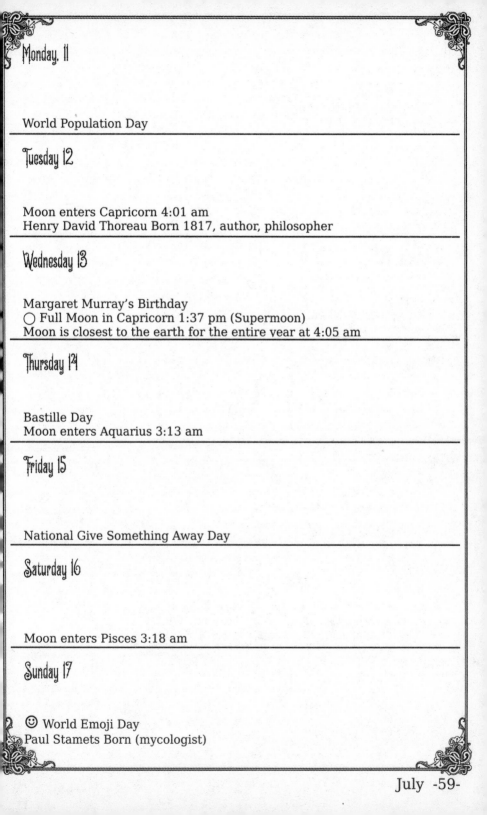

Monday, 11

World Population Day

Tuesday 12

Moon enters Capricorn 4:01 am
Henry David Thoreau Born 1817, author, philosopher

Wednesday 13

Margaret Murray's Birthday
○ Full Moon in Capricorn 1:37 pm (Supermoon)
Moon is closest to the earth for the entire year at 4:05 am

Thursday 14

Bastille Day
Moon enters Aquarius 3:13 am

Friday 15

National Give Something Away Day

Saturday 16

Moon enters Pisces 3:18 am

Sunday 17

☺ World Emoji Day
Paul Stamets Born (mycologist)

Monday, 18

Sea Day (Japan)
Moon enters Aries 6:17 am
Nelson Mandela Day

Tuesday 19

San Francisco Public Library Begins Lending Books 1880

Wednesday 20

Moon Day
◖ Last Quarter 9:18 am
Moon enters Taurus 1:22 pm

Thursday 21

Friday 22

Sun enters Leo 3:07 pm

Saturday 23

Moon enters Gemini 12:11 am
Air Force Colonel Eileen M. Collins becomes the
first woman to command a space shuttle. (1999)

Sunday 24

Parents Day
National Drive-Thru Day

Monday, 25

Moon enters Cancer 12:54 pm

Tuesday 26

National Bagelfest Day

Wednesday 27

Thursday 28

Moon enters Leo 1:36 am
Delta Aquarids Meteor Shower
● New Moon in Leo 12:54 pm

Friday 29

Delta Aquarids Meteor Shower

Saturday 30

Moon enters Virgo 1:10 pm
National Cheesecake Day
World (International) Friendship Day

Sunday 31

August

National Picnic Month, Water Quality Month

Mon	Tue	Wed	Thu	Fri	Sat	Sun
1 ❋	2 → ♎	3	4 → ♏	5 ◐	6 →⊕	7 ⊕
8 → ♑	9 ☿R	10 → ♒	11 ○♒	12 →∞	13	14 →♈
15	16 →♉	17	18 ◑	19 →♊	20	21 →♋
22 ☼→♍	23	24 →♌	25	26 →♍	27 ●♍	28
29 →♎	30	31 →♏				

Study Queues:

Runes-Elhaz, Sowilo **Tarot**-Temperance, Devil, the 4 eights **Botanicals**-Turmeric, Star Anise, Pennyroyal, Patchouli, Garlic, Goldenseal **Stones**-Ruby, Pyrite, Lodestone, Apatite **Deities**-Lugh, Heimdall, Zeus, THoth, Shango, Áine

August Lunar Planner

Mon	1	☽	✿
Tue	2	☽	
Wed	3	☽	
Thu	4	☽	
Fri	*5*	☽	
Sat	6	☽	
Sun	7	☽	⊕
Mon	8	☽	
Tue	9	☽	
Wed	10	☽	
Thu	*11*	☽	
Fri	12	☽	
Sat	13	☽	
Sun	14	☽	
Mon	15	☽	
Tue	16	☽	
Wed	17	☽	
Thu	*18*	☽	
Fri	19	☽	
Sat	20	☽	
Sun	21	☽	
Mon	22	☽	
Tue	23	☽	
Wed	24	☽	
Thu	25	☽	
Fri	26	☽	
Sat	*27*	☽	
Sun	28	☽	
Mon	29	☽	
Tue	30	☽	
Wed	31	☽	

Monday, August 1

Jerry Garcia Born
Sabbat: Lughnasadh/Imbolc, see page 97

Tuesday 2

National Coloring Book Day
Moon enters Libra 1:05 am

Wednesday 3

Grab Some Nuts Day

Thursday 4

Moon enters Scorpio 6:47 am

Friday 5

◗ First Quarter 6:06 am
The Mars Curiosity Rover celebrates the anniversary of its arrival by
singing the Happy Birthday Song to itself today, all alone, on Mars.

Saturday 6

Campfire Day (and Night)
Moon enters Sagittarius 11:38 pm

Sunday 7

Purple Heart Day
Exact Cross Quarter 7:36 am

Monday, 8

Moon enters Capricorn 1:39 pm
International Cat Day

Tuesday 9

National Book Lovers Day

Wednesday 10

Lazy Day
Smores Day
Moon enters Aquarius 1:45 pm

Thursday 11

Mountain Day (Japan)
○ Full Moon in Aquarius 8:35 pm

Friday 12

Perseids Meteor Shower
Moon enters Pisces 1:44 pm

Saturday 13

Perseids Meteor Shower
International Lefthanders Day
Hekate's Night / Artemis Night

Sunday 14

Moon enters Aries 3:43 pm

Monday, 15

Charles Godfrev Leland Born

Tuesday 16

National Rum Day
Moon enters Taurus 9:22 pm

Wednesday 17

National Thrift Shop Day
Black Cat Appreciation Day

Thursday 18

Bad Poetry Day
Serendipity Day
◑ Last Quarter 11:36 pm

Friday 19

National Aviation Day
Moon enters Gemini 7:06 am

Saturday 20

Tooth Fairy Day

Sunday 21

Senior Citizens Day
Moon enters Cancer 7:29 pm

Monday, 22

Sun enters Virgo 10:16 pm

Tuesday 23

Ride the Wind Day

Wednesday 24

Vesuvius Day
Moon enters Leo 8:09 am
National Waffle Day (U.S.)

Thursday 25

Friday 26

Women's Equality Day
Moon enters Virgo 7:24 pm

Saturday 27

Just Because Day
● New Moon in Virgo 3:17 am

Sunday 28

Monday, 29

Moon enters Libra 4:45 am

Tuesday 30

Mary Wollenstone Shelley Born 1818

Wednesday 31

Raymond Buckland Born
Moon enters Scorpio 12:11 pm

Thursday, September 1

Emma M. Nutt Day

Friday 2

Moon enters Sagittarius 5:39 pm

Saturday 3

◐ First Quarter 1:07 pm

Sunday 4

Moon enters Capricorn 9:02 pm
World Sexual Health Day

Weight & Volume Conversions

Unit [2]	Abbreviation	Equal To	fl oz	mL	Notes[3]
Drop	dr., gt., gtt.	1/96 t.	1/576	0.051 [4]	
1 mL	mL			1	~20 drops
Fluid Dram	fl.dr.	3/4 t.	1/8	3.69	~57 drops
Teaspoon	tsp. or t.	1/3 T	1/6	4.93	2 t.~10 mL
Tablespoon	tbsp. or T	1/16 C	1/2	14.79	~ 3 tsp.
Fluid Ounce (volume)	fl.oz. or oz.	1/8 C	1	29.57	2 tbsp.
Avoirdupois Ounce (weight)	oz.	28.3 grams	-	- [5]	
Cup	C	1/2 pint	8	236.59	2 C = 1 pt
Pint	pt.	1/2 qt	16	473.18	2 pt = 1 qt
Quart	qt.	1/4 gal	32	946.35	4 qt = 1 gal
Gallon	gal.	4 qt	128	3,785.41	

---

2   This table shows equivalents for volume measurements with the exception of the avoirdupois ounce. This exception is the only weight measurement with its gram (abbreviated "g") equivalent.

3   The tilde symbol is used to mean *approximately* or *about*. It is used here in a similar manner as ≈ is used to mean almost or approximately equal to. This is for general use rather than laboratory or mathematical use.

4   Depending on the material's viscosity, the dropper size, and other factors, a teaspoon has about 80 to 100 drops.

5   To approximate how many grams are in a measurement of mass, multiply the mass value by 28.35. Example, 2 ounces by weight is equal to 56.699 grams (2 x 28.35 = 56.699)

September

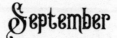

Civic Awareness Month, Wilderness Month, Courtesy Month, Chicken Month, Honey Month, Self-Improvement Month, Hispanic Heritage Month is Sept. 15-Oct. 15

Mon	Tue	Wed	Thu	Fri	Sat	Sun
			1	2 →⊕	3 ◑	4 →♑
5	6 →♒	7	8 →⠙	9	10 ○⠙	11 →♈
12	13 →♉	14	15 →♊	16	17 ◐	18 →♋
19	20 →♌	21	22 ✳ ☼→♎	23 →♍	24	25 →♎ ●♎
26	27 →♏	28	29 →⊕	30		

Study Queues:

Runes-Tiwaz, Berkano **Tarot**-Lovers, Star, the 4 nines **Botanicals**-Allspice, Dandelion, Willow, Ginseng, Ivy, House Leek **Stones**-Alexandrite, Sunstone, Kyanite, Selenite, Pearl **Deities**-Brân, Kvasir, Chaos, Arawn, Anten, Antenociticus, Min

September Lunar Planner

Thu	1	◑
Fri	2	◑
Sat	*3*	◑
Sun	4	◑
<u>**Mon**</u>	<u>**5**</u>	○
Tue	6	○
Wed	7	○
Thu	8	○
Fri	9	○
Sat	*10*	○
Sun	11	○
Mon	12	○
Tue	13	○
Wed	14	○
Thu	15	◐
Fri	16	◐
Sat	*17*	◐
Sun	18	◐
Mon	19	◐
Tue	20	◐
Wed	21	◐
Thu	22	◐ ❀
Fri	23	◐
Sat	24	●
Sun	*25*	●
Mon	26	●
Tue	27	◑
Wed	28	◑
Thu	29	◑
Fri	30	◑

Monday, 5

Crazy Horses Birthday
Labor Day (U.S. Federal) & Labour Day (Canadian National)

Tuesday 6

Moon enters Aquarius 10:41 pm

Wednesday 7

Independence Day (Brazil)

Thursday 8

International Literacy Day

Friday 9

☿R Mercury Retrograde
Moon enters Pisces 11:42 pm

Saturday 10

○ Full Moon in Pisces 4:59 am
Carl Llewelyn Weschcke Born

Sunday 11

Silver Ravenwolf Born
Moon enters Aries 1:47 am
National Grandparents Day

Monday, 12

Tuesday 13

Moon enters Taurus 6:39 am
International Programmers Day

Wednesday 14

Thursday 15

Make a Hat Day
Moon enters Gemini 3:16 pm

Friday 16

Independence Day (Mexico)
Constitution Day and Citizenship Day

Saturday 17

◑ Last Quarter 4:52 pm
National Clean Up Day
National POW/MIA Recognition Day

Sunday 18

Moon enters Cancer 2:59 am

Monday, 19

Talk Like a Pirate Day
Cecil Hugh Williamson Born
Respect for the Aged Day (Japan)

Tuesday 20

Moon enters Leo 3:37 pm

Wednesday 21

International Day of Peace

Thursday 22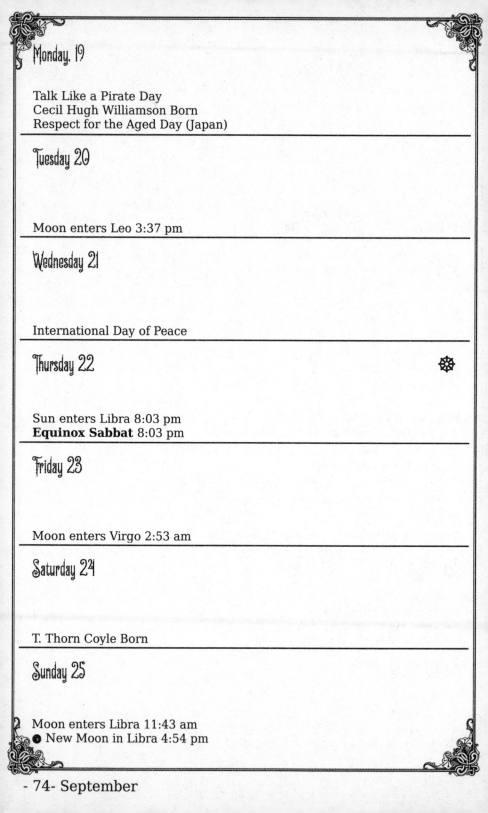

Sun enters Libra 8:03 pm
Equinox Sabbat 8:03 pm

Friday 23

Moon enters Virgo 2:53 am

Saturday 24

T. Thorn Coyle Born

Sunday 25

Moon enters Libra 11:43 am
● New Moon in Libra 4:54 pm

Monday, 26

Tuesday 27

World Tourism Day
Moon enters Scorpio 6:14 pm

Wednesday 28

Thursday 29

World Heart Day
Moon enters Sagittarius 11:03 pm

Friday 30

National Mud Pack Day
National Hot Mulled Cider Day

Saturday, October 1

Isaac Bonewits Born
World Vegetarian Day
International Coffee Day
International Observe the Moon Night

Sunday 2

☿ Mercury Direct
Mahatma Gandhi Born
◑ First Quarter 7:14 pm
Moon enters Capricorn 2:37 am

October

Domestic Violence Awareness Month, Breast Cancer Awareness Month,
Diversity Awareness Month, Black History Month (UK)

Mon	Tue	Wed	Thu	Fri	Sat	Sun
					1	2 ☽ ☿Direct →♑
3	4 →♒	5	6 →♋	7	8 →♈	9 ○♈
10 →♉	11	12	13 →♊	14	15 →♋	16
17 ◑	18 →♌	19	20 →♍	21	22 →♎	23 ☼→♏
24	25 →♏ ●♏	26	27 →♐	28	29 →♑	30
31 ✾ →♒						

Study Queues: **Runes**-Ehwaz, Mannaz **Tarot**-Moon, Sun, the 4 tens
Botanicals-Angelica, Calendula, Comfrey, Dill, High John the Conqueror,
Lemongrass **Stones**-Opal, Amber, Jet, Coral, Abalone, Paua **Deities**-Ód,
Aphrodite, Camulus, Arnemetia, Jarilo, Manabozho

October Lunar Planner

Sat	1	◗
Sun	*2*	◗
Mon	3	◗
Tue	4	◖
Wed	5	◯
Thu	6	◯
Fri	7	◯
Sat	8	◯
Sun	*9*	◯
<u>**Mon**</u>	<u>**10**</u>	◯
Tue	11	◯
Wed	12	◖
Thu	13	◖
Fri	14	◖
Sat	15	◖
Sun	16	◖
Mon	*17*	◖
Tue	18	◖
Wed	19	◖
Thu	20	◖
Fri	21	●
Sat	22	●
Sun	23	●
Mon	24	●
Tue	*25*	●
Wed	26	●
Thu	27	◗
Fri	28	◗
Sat	29	◗
Sun	30	◗
Mon	31	◗ ✿

Monday, 3

Child Health Day

Tuesday 4

Moon enters Aquarius 5:20 am

Wednesday 5

World Teachers Day

Thursday 6

Moon enters Pisces 7:47 am

Friday 7

Arnold Crowther Born
Draconids Meteor Shower

Saturday 8

Moon enters Aries 10:56 am
Draconids Meteor Shower

Sunday 9

Leif Erikson Day
○ Full Moon in Aries 3:54 pm

Monday, 10

Columbus Day (U.S. Federal)
Indigenous Peoples Day
Moon enters Taurus 4:03 pm
Thanksgiving Day (Canada)

Tuesday 11

Wednesday 12

Farmers Day
Childrens Day (Brazil)

Thursday 13

Moon enters Gemini 12:08 am

Friday 14

Patricia Crowther Born

Saturday 15

Sweetest Day
White Cane Safety Day
Moon enters Cancer 11:11 pm
International Day of Rural Women

Sunday 16

Boss's Day
World Food Day

Monday, 17

◑ Last Quarter 12:15 pm

Tuesday 18

Moon enters Leo 11:44 am

Wednesday 19

Thursday 20

Selena Fox Born
Moon enters Virgo 11:25 pm

Friday 21

Orionids Meteor Shower

Saturday 22

Orionids Meteor Shower
Moon enters Libra 8:24 pm

Sunday 23

Gertrude Ederle Birthday
Sun enters Scorpio 5:36 am

Monday, 24

United Nations Day
Labour Day (New Zealand)

Tuesday 25

Moon enters Scorpio 2:18 am
● New Moon in Scorpio 5:48 am
Partial Solar Eclipse 3:58 am
World Pasta Day | International Artist Day

Wednesday 26

National Pumpkin Day

Thursday 27

National Black Cat Day
Moon enters Sagittarius 5:54 am

Friday 28

National Chocolate Day

Saturday 29

Hermit Day
Moon enters Capricorn 8:21 am

Sunday 30

National Candy Corn Day

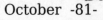

November

Native American Heritage Month, Epilepsy Month, Diabetes Awareness Month, Adoption Awareness Month, Caregivers Appreciation Month. November 8th is a total lunar eclipse.

Mon	Tue	Wed	Thu	Fri	Sat	Sun
	1 ☽	2 →♒	3	4 →♈	5	6 →♉
7 ⊕	8 ○♉	9 →♊	10	**11** →♋	12	13
14 →♌	15	16 ☽ →♍	17	18	19 →♎	20
21 →♏	22 ☀→♐ →♐ ●♐	23	**24**	25 →♑	26	27 →♒
28	29 →♒	30 ☽				

Study Queues:
Runes-Laguz, Ingwaz **Tarot**-Judgment, the 4 Pages **Botanicals**-Damiana, Scullcap, Caraway, Marjoram, Nutmeg, Mandrake, Cayenne
Stones-Bloodstone, Moss Agate, Carnelian, Fire Opal
Deities-Hecate, Ra, Hades, Rhiannon, Gitche, Manitou, Pele

November Lunar Planner

Tue	*1*	◐
Wed	2	◐
Thu	3	◖
Fri	4	◖
Sat	5	◖
Sun	6	◯
Mon	7	◯ ⊕
Tue	*8*	◯
Wed	9	◯
Thu	10	◯
Fri	**11**	◗
Sat	12	◗
Sun	13	◗
Mon	14	◗
Tue	15	◑
Wed	*16*	◑
Thu	17	◐
Fri	18	●
Sat	19	●
Sun	20	●
Mon	21	●
Tue	*22*	●
Wed	23	●
Thu	**24**	●
Fri	25	●
Sat	26	◐
Sun	27	◐
Mon	28	◐
Tue	29	◐
Wed	*30*	◐

Monday, 31

Sabbat: Samhain/Beltane, see page 97
Halloween (secular holiday)
Moon enters Aquarius 10:43 am

Tuesday, November 1

◐ First Quarter 1:37 am
Day of the Dead
Samhain Continues

Wednesday 2

Moon enters Pisces 1:46 pm

Thursday 3

Sandwich Day
Culture Day (Japan)

Friday 4

Taurids Meteor Shower
Moon enters Aries 6:07 pm

Saturday 5

Guy Fawkes Day & Night
National Love Your Red Hair Day

Sunday 6

New York City Marathon
Moon enters Taurus 11:14 pm
Daylight Saving Time ends 2:00 am Set Clocks back -1 hour (U.S.)

Monday, 7

⊕

Exact Cross Quarter 4:36 am

Tuesday 8

National Cappuccino Day
Election Day (U.S.) Please Vote!
Total Lunar Eclipse 2:02 am
○ Full Moon in Taurus 5:02 am

Wednesday 9

World Freedom Day
Moon enters Gemini 7:37 am

Thursday 10

World Science Day for Peace and Development

Friday 11

Moon enters Cancer 6:22 pm
Remembrance Day (Canadian)
Veterans Day (U.S. Federal)

Saturday 12

Sunday 13

World Kindness Day

Monday. 14

National Pickle Day
Moon enters Leo 6:48 am

Tuesday 15

Revolution Day (Mexico)

Wednesday 16

◑ Last Quarter 7:27 am
International Day of Tolerance
Moon enters Virgo 7:03 pm

Thursday 17

Israel Regardie Born
Leonids Meteor Shower
World Philosophy Day

Friday 18

Saturday 19

Moon enters Libra 4:57 am

Sunday 20

Revolution Day Memorial (Mexico)

Monday, 21

World Hello Day
World Television Day
Moon enters Scorpio 11:16 pm
Revolution Day Memorial Observed (Mexico)

Tuesday 22

Go For a Ride Day
Sun enters Sagittarius 2:21 am

Wednesday 23

Labor Thanksgiving Day (Japan)
Moon enters Sagittarius 2:15 pm
National Espresso Day
● New Moon in Sagittarius 4:57 pm

Thursday 24

Thanksgiving Day (U.S. Federal)

Friday 25

Black Friday
Buy Nothing Day
Moon enters Capricorn 3:18 pm

Saturday 26

Sunday 27

Moon enters Aquarius 4:07 pm

December

Bingo Month, Write to a Friend Month

Mon	Tue	Wed	Thu	Fri	Sat	Sun
			1 →♈	2	3	4 →♉
5	6 →♊	7 ○♊	8	9 →♋	10	11 →♌
12	13	14 →♍	15	16 ◐ →♎	17	18 →♏
19	20	21 ❄ ☀→♑ →⊕	22	23 →♑ ●♑	24	**25** →♒
26	27 →♒	28	29 ◑ ☿℞ →♈	30	31 →♉	January 1, 2023 ☿ Direct

Study Queues:

Runes-Dagaz, Othala **Tarot**-World, the 4 Queens, the 4 Kings **Botanicals**-Parsley, Verbena, Fern, Agrimony, Fennel, Cumin
Stones-Sodalite, Zircon, Topaz, Turquoise
Deities-Artemis, Fer Doirich, Aengus, Anubis, Chac, Eingana

December Lunar Planner

Thu	1	◐
Fri	2	◐
Sat	3	◑
Sun	4	◑
Mon	5	◯
Tue	6	◯
Wed	*7*	◯
Thu	8	◯
Fri	9	◯
Sat	10	◗
Sun	11	◗
Mon	12	◗
Tue	13	◗
Wed	14	◖
Thu	15	◖
Fri	*16*	◖
Sat	17	◖
Sun	18	◗
Mon	19	◗
Tue	20	◗
Wed	21	● ✵
Thu	22	●
Fri	*23*	●
Sat	24	●
<u>**Sun**</u>	<u>**25**</u>	◖
<u>**Mon**</u>	<u>**26**</u>	◖
Tue	27	◖
Wed	28	◖
Thu	*29*	◖
Fri	30	◐
Sat	31	◑

Monday, 28

Cyber Monday
National French Toast Day

Tuesday 29

Square Dance Day
Moon enters Pisces 6:15 pm

Wednesday 30

◑ First Quarter 8:36 am

Thursday, December 1

Moon enters Aries 10:41 pm
Rosa Parks Day (Ohio, Alabama, Oregon)
First military grave marker with a pentacle allowed for veterans in 2007

Friday 2

Saturday 3

Sunday 4

International Cookie Day
Moon enters Taurus 5:38 am

Monday, 5

World Soil Day
International Volunteer Day
Repeal (of Prohibition) Day

Tuesday 6

Moon enters Gemini 1:48 pm

Wednesday 7

○ Full Moon in Gemini 10:08 pm

Thursday 8

Friday 9

Moon enters Cancer 1:49 am
Sarah "Tabitha" Babbitt Born (tool maker and inventor)

Saturday 10

Human Rights Day

Sunday 11

International Mountain Day
Moon enters Leo 2:08 pm

Monday, 12

Gingerbread House Day

Tuesday 13

National Cocoa Day
Geminids Meteor Shower

Wednesday 14

Moon enters Virgo 2:45 am

Thursday 15

Bill of Rights Day
Friday Gladheart Born

Friday 16

◑ Last Quarter 2:56 am
Moon enters Libra 1:49 pm

Saturday 17

Wright Brothers Day

Sunday 18

Hanukkah Begins
Moon enters Scorpio 9:30 pm

Monday, 19

Ronald Hutton Born

Tuesday 20

Wednesday 21

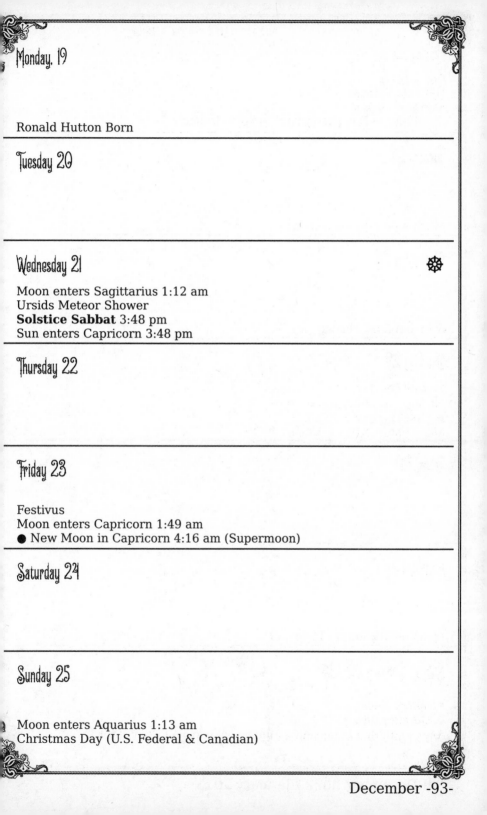

Moon enters Sagittarius 1:12 am
Ursids Meteor Shower
Solstice Sabbat 3:48 pm
Sun enters Capricorn 3:48 pm

Thursday 22

Friday 23

Festivus
Moon enters Capricorn 1:49 am
● New Moon in Capricorn 4:16 am (Supermoon)

Saturday 24

Sunday 25

Moon enters Aquarius 1:13 am
Christmas Day (U.S. Federal & Canadian)

Monday, 26

Boxing Day
Hanukkah Ends
Kwanzaa Begins
St. Stephens Day (National Holiday in Ireland)

Tuesday 27

Moon enters Pisces 1:34 am

Wednesday 28

National Card Playing Day

Thursday 29

Pepper Pot Day
☿℞ Mercury Retrograde
◐ First Quarter 7:20 pm
Moon enters Aries 4:36 am

Friday 30

Saturday 31

Moon enters Taurus 11:08 pm

Sunday, January 1, 2023

Kwanzaa Ends
☿ Mercury Direct
Any month that begins on a Sunday will have a Friday the 13th

The Witches' Sabbats

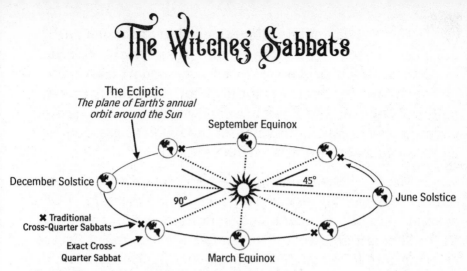

The earth's orbit around the sun can be visualized as an orbital plane (known as the ecliptic) that is divided into eight sections.

Sabbats are times of the year noted by Witches for their powerful magical energy, celestial symmetry, and spiritual significance. The image above shows that the two Solstices and two Equinoxes fall 90° apart from each other and divide the earth's orbit around the sun into quarters. These Solstices (Summer and Winter) and Equinoxes (Vernal[6] and Autumnal) are referred to as **Quarter Sabbats**.

Cross-Quarter Sabbats fall between the Quarter Sabbats and have specific dates of celebration that have been drawn from historical reconstruction or specific Pagan or Wiccan Traditions. **Celebrations usually begin the evening before the Sabbat date.**

> **Imbolc - February 2**
> **Beltane - May 1**
> **Lughnasadh - August 1**
> **Samhain - November 1.**

---

6   Vernal means Spring.

The midway points along the ecliptic between each Solstice and Equinox are the **_Exact_ _Cross-Quarter Sabbats_** (Astrological Sabbat dates). Exact Cross-Quarter Sabbats are 90° apart from each other on the ecliptic and fall precisely half-way between the Equinoxes and Solstices. The traditional Cross-Quarters fall slightly before the Exact Cross-Quarters dates as indicated by ✖ in image on the previous page.

Many Witches combine the traditional Cross-Quarter Sabbat dates with the modern Exact Cross-Quarters. For example, traditional Samhain celebrations begin on October 31st and continue through November 1st. The Exact Cross-Quarter date for Samhain is November 7th. This is when the earth is 45° between the time/place of the Autumnal Equinox and the Winter Solstice. Some Witches celebrate Samhain from October 31st though November 7th.

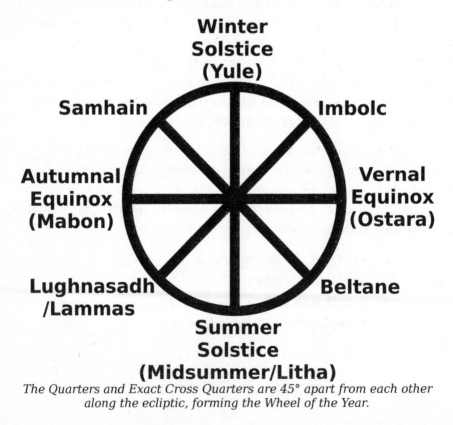

The Quarters and Exact Cross Quarters are 45° apart from each other along the ecliptic, forming the Wheel of the Year.

Northern & Southern Hemispheres

Solstices, Equinoxes, and Exact Cross-Quarters are precise astronomical events. These Sabbats do not fall on the same calendar day every year. The tables on the following pages provide a quick reference for these Sabbats in various time zones. Traditional dates for the Cross-Quarters are noted under their common name in the left column. Additional time zone conversions can be found on pages 12-13.

Which Sabbat you celebrate on a particular date depends on your tradition and location. Witches in the Southern Hemisphere (SH) sometimes follow the traditional Northern Hemisphere (NH) Sabbats according to their training and studies. These practitioners celebrate Samhain in October as do most UK and U.S. traditions.

However, it can be difficult to prepare for a harvest Sabbat such as Samhain when it is early spring outside your door. While it is Autumn in the NH at this time, it is spring in the SH. It makes sense that some choose to celebrate the Sabbats according to the current local season. Seasonal Sabbat dates for the SH can be found on page 99.

Many SH initiates begin their practice by following the NH Wheel according to their training but, may switch to the SH Wheel once they move from studying into regular practice. For these SH Witches, Sabbats are on the opposite sides of the Wheel just like the hemispheres are opposite each other.

The Wheel of the Year on page 3 has the Sabbat dates for both the Northern and Southern Hemispheres.

Remember, **you** are the final authority in your practice! You have the final say in which Sabbats you celebrate and at what time of the year you do so.

2022 Sabbat Times & Dates Northern Hemisphere

This table shows all the traditional Sabbat dates, Exact Cross-Quarter Sabbat dates, Equinox Sabbats, and Solstice Sabbats.

Sabbat Names *Traditional Date*	Astronomical Sabbat Dates & Times			
	Pacific	Central	Eastern	GMT
Imbolc ❁ *February 2*	⊕ **February 3**			
	12:37 pm	2:37 pm	3:37 pm	8:37 pm
Vernal Equinox /Ostara	❁ **March 20**			
	8:33 am	*10:33 am*	*11:33 am*	3:33 pm
Beltane ❁ *May 1*	⊕ **May 5**			
	5:25 am	*7:25 am*	*8:25 am*	12:25 pm
Summer Solstice/Litha/ Midsummer	❁ **June 21**			
	2:13 am	*4:13 am*	*5:13 am*	9:13 am
Lughnasadh ❁ *August 1*	⊕ **August 7**			
	5:36 am	*7:36 am*	*8:36 am*	12:36 pm
Autumnal Equinox/Mabon	❁ **September 22**			**Sept. 23**
	6:03 pm	8:03 pm	9:03 pm	1:03 am
Samhain ❁ *October 31 - November 1*	⊕ **November 7**			
	2:36 am	4:36 am	5:36 am	10:35 am
❁ **Winter Solstice /Yule**	❁ **December 21**			
	1:48 pm	3:48 pm	4:48 pm	9:48 pm

❁ Traditional Sabbat Date   ⊕ Exact Cross Quarter Sabbat Date

2022 Sabbat Times & Dates Southern Hemisphere

This table follows the seasonal dates of Sabbats. See page 97 for more information about Sabbats in the Southern Hemisphere.

Sabbat Names *Traditional Date*	Astronomical Sabbat Dates & Times			
	Pacific	Central	Eastern	GMT
Lughnasadh ❁ *February 2*	⊕ **February 3**			
	12:37 pm	2:37 pm	3:37 pm	8:37 pm
Autumnal Equinox/Mabon	❁ **March 20**			
	8:33 am	*10:33 am*	*11:33 am*	3:33 pm
Samhain ❁ *October 31 - November 1*	⊕ **May 5**			
	5:25 am	*7:25 am*	*8:25 am*	12:25 pm
Winter Solstice /Yule	❁ **June 21**			
	2:13 am	*4:13 am*	*5:13 am*	9:13 am
Imbolc ❁ *August 1*	⊕ **August 7**			
	5:36 am	*7:36 am*	*8:36 am*	12:36 pm
Vernal Equinox /Ostara	❁ **September 22**			Sept. 23
	6:03 pm	*8:03 pm*	*9:03 pm*	1:03 am
Beltane ❁ *May 1*	⊕ **November 7**			
	2:36 am	*4:36 am*	*5:36 am*	10:35 am
Summer Solstice/Litha/ Midsummer	❁ **December 21**			
	1:48 pm	3:48 pm	4:48 pm	9:48 pm

Daylight Savings Time is already calculated for times in *italics*.

Eclipse Times & Magic

Your almanac notes the *Eclipse Begins* time in the tables on the next few pages. This is the first moment the shadow touches the earth. If an eclipse is visible in your area, the best viewing will be close to the *Peak Time* noted in the table. **An eclipse doesn't have to be visible for you to be able to work with its energy.** You can use the begin and end times as the window in which you might work your magic.

There is a moment of apparent hesitation when a pendulum reaches the edge of the arc in its swing before it reverses back. The energy of an eclipse is similar to this, and sensitive Witches may feel this as a time of anticipation and suspended time. Eclipses provide us with an opportunity to work interesting varieties of magic.

Working with Lunar Eclipse Energies

Throughout the moon's cycle, its light waxes and wanes. During a lunar eclipse the moon's light waxes and wanes in a way that is similar to its usual phases. The moon is always in its full phase when a lunar eclipse occurs, but as it becomes partially or completely hidden and then visible again the energy cycles through its waning and waxing phases within a short period of time.

In addition to this cyclical energy, we become acutely aware of the earth's presence. The earth's shadow falls across the moon as she comes into position between the moon and the sun. This causes a unification of earth and moon energy, reinforcing the sense of wholeness and the completion of cycles. You might find this an excellent time to focus on the Goddess, work on your psychic skills, perform divination, or charge a special eclipse moon water (see page 146).

When planning your magic for a lunar eclipse, consider the primary full moon energy first. As the eclipse begins, you might work with waning moon energy. At the peak of the lunar eclipse, shift your focus to goals associated with the new or dark moon. As the eclipse ends, you are working with waxing moon energy again. Once the eclipse is over, you are back to full moon energy.

Lunar Eclipses of 2022

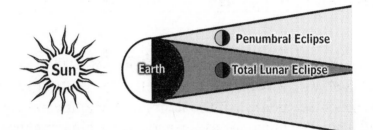

When the moon is entirely within the earth's shadow it is a total lunar eclipse. A partial lunar eclipse occurs when the *umbra* (Latin for *shadow*) appears to take a bite out of a part of the moon. A penumbral eclipse (*pen* is from the Latin *pœne* for *nearly* or *almost*) occurs when the diffuse outer shadow of the earth falls on the moon's surface. This year we will experience two total lunar eclipses.

May 15–16 Total Lunar Eclipse

Visible to all of North and South America, southwest areas of Europe, Asia, and Africa. Areas in the northwest United States may only see a partial eclipse (in the penumbra).

Event	UTC Time	Central Time
Eclipse Begins	May 16- 01:32	May 15- 8:32 pm
Peak Time	May 16- 04:11	May 15- 11:11 pm
Eclipse Ends	May 16- 06:51	May 16- 1:51 am

Nov 8 Total Lunar Eclipse

Completely visible in most of the North and Western United States, and partially visible to the rest of North America and almost all but the far Eastern coast of South America. Visible in Australia, North and East areas of Europe, and Asia.

Event	UTC Time	Central Time
Eclipse Begins	08:02	2:02 am
Peak Time	10:59	4:59 am
Eclipse Ends	13:56	7:56 am

Working with Solar Eclipse Energies

Daylight hours increase after the Winter Solstice until the Summer Solstice when the hours of daylight wane again. During a solar eclipse, we experience something similar to a micro year. The sun is whole, then partially or completely hidden, and then visible again. Within just a few minutes, an energy similar to a complete cycle of solstices and equinoxes can be felt, while at the same time we become highly aware of the moon's presence. Her shadow falls across the earth as she comes into position between the earth and the sun. Solar and lunar energy is united, reinforcing the sense of wholeness and the completion of cycles.

When planning your magic to be harmonious with a solar eclipse, consider that a solar eclipse can only occur during the day on a new moon. This means that you are working with new moon energy. At the beginning of a solar eclipse, you could focus on ridding yourself of unwanted energies, bad habits, unhealthy patterns of thinking and acting, negativity, and other baneful things in your life. As the eclipse passes you could bring into your focus the things you wish to increase and grow in your life such as prosperity, positive thoughts and actions, and good health.

Solar Eclipses of 2022

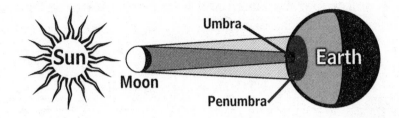

When the moon is near apogee it is farther away from the earth. During an eclipse it appears smaller, leaving a thin ring of the sun uncovered. This causes an annular eclipse as shown in the illustration to the right. During a total eclipse, the moon is near perigee (close to the earth). It appears larger and covers the entire sun causing a total solar eclipse. A partial solar eclipse occurs when the sun and moon are not in a straight line to each other and only the penumbra falls on the earth. This year there are two partial solar eclipses.

Apr 30 Partial Solar Eclipse

Most of the umbra covers the Atlantic, Antarctic, and Pacific oceans, but some areas of Argentina, Bolivia, and Chili will be in the penumbra.

Event	UTC Time	Central Time
Eclipse Begins	8:45	1:45 pm
Peak Time	20:42	3:42 pm
Eclipse Ends	22:38	5:38 pm

Oct 25 Partial Solar Eclipse

Visible in Europe, the North and East areas of Africa, and the South and West areas of Asia.

Event	UTC Time	Central Time
Eclipse Begins	08:58	3:58 am
Peak Time	11:00	6:00 am
Eclipse Ends	13:02	8:02 am

World Events this Year

U.S. November 8 – The 2022 U.S. elections will select the 118th Congress, the first after redistricting that reflects the 2020 U.S. Census. This is a critical year! Please make sure you are registered to vote early as there are several new restrictive voting laws in many areas. Keeping our religious freedoms is dependent upon your vote. If you are unable to vote, consider donating your time or money to important causes. Visit Vote.org for help with registration, vote reminders, poll locations, and other assistance.

Germany is schedule to phase out nuclear energy.

India is set to launch humans into space in 2022, becoming the fourth nation to do so, joining Russia, the U.S. and China.

England is scheduled to open Europe's largest transportation projects ever. Crossrail, a new rail built for southeast England and London, has been in development since 1974.

Perigee & Apogee

When the moon is at perigee (pĕr'ə-jē) it is closest to the earth in orbit. Apogee (ăp'ə-jē) is when the moon is farthest away in its orbit. The closest distance for the entire year is July 13th at 4:05 am, and the farthest distance for the entire year is on June 29th at 1:08 am as shown in *italics* below.

Perigee Dates	Time	Apogee Dates	Time
January 1	4:55 pm	January 14	3:25 am
January 30	1:11 am	February 10	8:37 pm
February 26	4:25 pm	March 10	5:03 pm
March 23	6:37 pm	April 7	2:10 pm
April 19	10:13 am	May 5	7:46 am
May 17	10:27 am	June 1	8:13 pm
June 14	6:23 pm	*June 29*	*1:08 am*
July 13	*4:05 am*	July 26	5:21 am
August 10	12:08 pm	August 22	4:52 pm
September 7	1:18 pm	September 19	9:43 am
October 4	11:33 am	October 17	5:19 am
October 29	9:35 am	November 14	12:40 am
November 25	7:31 pm	December 11	6:28 pm
December 24	2:26 am		

Supermoons & Micromoons

A supermoon occurs when a full or new moon coincides with perigee. In 2022, there are two super full moons and two super new moons. A micromoon occurs when a full or new moon coincides with apogee such as on June 28.

Jan 2	Super New Moon	Jul 13	Super Full Moon
Jun 14	Super Full Moon	Dec 23	Super New Moon
Jun 28	Micro New Moon		

Black & Blue Moons

There are two types of blue moons and three types of black moons. There are no blue moons under either definition in 2022[7], but there are three black moons.

A Seasonal Black or Blue Moon is the third new (black) or full (blue) moon of an astronomical season in which there are four new or full moons. An astrological season is the time period between the quarter Sabbats (solstices and equinoxes).

A Monthly Black or Blue Moon is the second new or full moon in a calendar month with two new or full moons.

February Black Moons happen about once every 19 years. This is when there is either no full or no new moon during the month of February. Time zone differences mean that this last type of black moon is not necessarily a worldwide event. This year is a February black new moon because there is not a new moon in the calendar month.

Black Moon Magic in 2022

There are three black moons in 2022, a rare occurrence. As mentioned above, February has no new moon so it is called a black moon month. The other two black moons are monthly black moons. The first is on January 31 at 11:46 pm, and the second in on April 30 at 3:28 pm.

The time of the black moon will amplify the energies of renewal, rebirth, transformation, and change. It is also a very powerful time for banishing, cleansing, exorcism, hex-reversal, un-crossing, and purification. Working with these energies on January 31st, all of February, and on April 30th will add extra power to your intentions.

---

7 The next blue moon will be the seasonal type, on August 19, 2024.

Gratitude Ritual (and Happiness Spell)

Try a gratitude ritual to help you achieve happiness, well-being, optimism, increased energy, mental balance, better tolerance, reduced frustration, and increased self-confidence. This spell works through both valid psychological techniques and magical principles. Give it a shot, you'll be grateful.

Timing Your Spell: For this spell you will be creating a powerfully charged talisman you can carry with you. Begin your spell during the waxing moon such as on the day of the first quarter moon. Complete the spell on the full moon. The effects of this spell will be evident to most practitioners within just a couple of days, but continued focus of your will and intent for at least a week can result in greater success.

Select a Talisman: You can use any object that is easily carried such as a stone, crystal, or piece of jewelry. The picture on the next page shows a few items to inspire you. The acorn is a brass finial I nabbed from the top of a lamp after being inspired by an episode of Bewitched! I used the iron key from my mother's oak dresser in the picture because it already triggered fond memories. Your favorite pentacle or triquetra necklace, a clear quartz crystal, a tumble-polished rose quartz, lapis lazuli, moonstone, or smooth landscaping rock will all do nicely. Once you have completed the spell, your talisman is imbued with power. Holding it will increase your happiness and energy and it can help you to put stressful situations into perspective for better problem-solving.

Charging Your Talisman: The directions for this working are shockingly simple. Every day, hold the object you have chosen and focus on one thing that you are grateful for. Of course, you may repeat the exercise throughout the day whenever you think of something. If you carry the talisman in your pocket you can just touch it while you focus your intent. Close your eyes and feel the gratitude you have and send it through your hand into the talisman. Truly feel your thankfulness and gratitude. Don't allow guilt or a sense of indebtedness creep into your thoughts or emotions. This isn't about owing back, it's about true appreciation, acknowledging and accepting.

You may speak Words of Power or a prayer of thanks to your chosen deities/deity at the end of your energy projection, but sometimes the deep sense of gratitude may overwhelm you to the point that there are no words to express it. You may just end the focusing session with 'so mote it be' or an affirmation.

On the last day of your spell, think about how the energy of the full moon reflects the fullness of your gratitude. You may choose to leave your talisman out under the energy of the full moon this night. It doesn't matter if it is cloudy, the full moon will still imbue your talisman with energy. If you have selected an item that should not be left outdoors, just leave it on a windowsill or your altar.

Carry your talisman with you whenever you need a mental or spiritual lift. As the year progresses, you may wish to boost the energy of your talisman by repeating your focus during any moon phase. You might discover that making this a daily ritual can be very rewarding.

*An assortment of items that
can be used for gratitude rituals.*

Critical Thinking

A fallacy is a type of persuasion used to sell you a product, idea, political stance, or simply to win a debate. Sharpening your ability to understand these tricks of logic will help in handling everything from the daily news and social media to your spiritual endeavors. There is never a shortage of cults, snake oil salesmen, and politicians, but this list of logical fallacies may help you avoid some of their tricks.[8]

Ignoratio Elenchi (Irrelevant Conclusion)

Also known as the Red Herring, Straw Man. This fallacy is about distraction and diversion, like a devious stage magician showing you a shiny trinket while he picks your pocket. The conclusions of a statement miss the point. They may be valid and logical, but they are off-topic or irrelevant.

"Dogs are too cute to be dangerous." Sure, they may be cute, but that does not predicate their harmlessness. Diversion tactics are frequently used to keep the focus of an argument on an emotionally charged topic, regardless of if that is the main topic at hand.

Argumentum ad hominem (Insulting Someone's Character)

This fallacy attacks a person rather than the subject at hand. The usual approach comes as a personal attack on the person or the questioning their credentials, skills, and expertise. "Pat says that this restaurant is good, but they're vegan so we can't trust that recommendation." Maybe Pat is vegan, but that doesn't mean the restaurant isn't good, just that it has vegan options that are tasty.

---

8   There are different schools of thought regarding the categorization of logical fallacies, and some of those listed here are closely related. The format presented is designed for clarity and quick understanding.

Petitio principii (Begging the Question)

This is a circular argument where an assumption is used as proof. "My house is haunted because it has cold spots." The conclusion (haunted) is assumed as true and may or may not have anything to do with the cold spots.

Non sequitur

Also known as *derailment* or *that doesn't follow*, and closely related to Ignoratio Elenchi, this fallacy asks you to make jumps in your logic. The conclusion has nothing to do with the evidental statements. "Witches use herbs. You can see it all over Instagram. Plants are clearly put here as a temptation from Satan." See how quickly that logic train derailed? There is no logical progression to the conclusion.

Post hoc ergo propter hoc (after this, therefore because of this)

There is an assumption that an event is the cause of a later event, or *false cause and effect*. "Every time I wear this shirt my sports team wins the game. I'm wearing it Saturday, so you can count on a win." Most often you see this fallacy in the form of someone assuming causation where there may be just a correlation.

Argumentum ad populum (Bandwagoning)

Because most people believe something is true, it is asserted that it must be true or valid. "Everyone calls Alex a *her*, so that must be the pronoun Alex uses." It is best to simply ask Alex instead of going with the group consensus in this situation.

Either-Or Fallacy (false dichotomy)

This is a false dilemma constructed when a situation is oversimplified. You might be presented with two mutually exclusive subjects, or be given a choice between something obvious and something ludicrous. "You are either vegan or you hate the environment." "If you want to be good at tarot, you will buy this deck."

Card Stacking (Cherry Picking)

In media this is known as "controlling the message" and it is a technique where only select evidence is used to support an assertion. Contrary evidence is withheld or diminished. This is expected when a job resume contains cherry-picked evidence demonstrating a person's qualifications for a job, but it can be taken to an extreme. "Fifteen military generals support this." But, how many do not support it?

False Equivalence and False Analogy

Asserting that two or more things are equivalent. "Mint and belladonna are both plants, and plant-based diets are healthy so we should include these plants in our diets." Belladonna is quite poisonous and is certainly not the same as mint just because it is a plant.

Hasty Generalization (Converse Accident)

This fallacy happens when a general rule is created because a conclusion was reached by observing a few atypical examples. "Did you see in the paper where that yoga instructor was accused of pedophilia? Those yogis are all a bunch of evildoers!"

Pentagram   **Pentacle**

There is much debate over the terms pentagram and pentacle. Although many use the terms interchangeably, the currently accepted standard is that a pentagram is a geometric shape and a pentacle is a talisman such as a pendant.

Watch the Witch News

Pay close attention when you are reading newspapers and internet articles that involve under-represented faiths. The use of language in the media is a huge tip-off to a writer's or news outlet's perspective. Stay alert for words like "self-proclaimed" and "reportedly". You've probably seen articles with this type of copy, "Whats-her-name, a self-proclaimed Witch, tells us that..." Read that again, but this time substitute the word "Witch" with "Christian", "Muslim" or "Jew". It's ridiculous, isn't it?

When you see "reportedly", take note of the message being conveyed "The area is reportedly popular among occultists." Reported by whom? Who is the source?

How many times have you seen a reporter covering a local coven for a lifestyle article near Halloween? The reporter may interview a Christian pastor for "their views about Witchcraft". Imagine if this situation were reversed and the nightly news interviewed the local Witches to discover "their take" on the local "self-proclaimed" Christian who "reportedly" holds Sunday services.

2022 Practical Herb Award: Rosemary

(*Rosmarinus officinalis*) Rosemary is an excellent multi-purpose herb to have on hand. It is used in magic for purification, strength, blessing, protection, improving memory, and love. It has a wide array of culinary uses and will grow in USDA Hardiness Zones 1 through 9. It is inexpensive, easily obtained, and its anti-inflammatory and anti-microbial properties are utilized in food, cosmetics, and herbal remedies.

The Simpler's Method

       Sometimes you will come across a recipe written in the *apothecary style*. This style of recipe uses the traditional *simpler's method*, giving you the flexibility of *parts*. A *part* can be a measurement of weight or volume. When parts are used in a recipe, there should be some indication of whether the part is by weight or volume.

Parts by Volume

       When a recipe uses parts by volume, you use a liquid measurement. For small recipes you might make a teaspoon your volume part. Larger recipes can be made by using a fluid ounce, a cup, or a quart as your part measurement.

Parts by Weight

       Recipes for parts by weight require a scale. For small recipes you might use a gram as your part. Larger recipes can be created by using ounces or pounds for your part.

Ritual Altar Incense

       This is a loose incense to use on charcoal incense disks. It is an all-purpose altar incense that works for any magical purpose such as cleansing, meditation, manifestation, blessings, etc. Parts (pt) are by volume. Use a half teaspoon for your part measurement to make a small batch. Resins should be broken up in your mortar and pestle into approximately uniform pieces about the size of rice.

      2 pt Frankincense - 4 pt White Copal - 1 pt Myrrh
      2 pt Rosemary Leaves - 2 pt Lavender Flowers

Making Self-Lighting Incense Powders

For 24 years the almanac has provided loose incense recipes for use over charcoal such as the one on the previous page. For this anniversary edition it's time to go pro with some self-lighting incense powders.

This type of incense is a powder that you form into a tall pile about the size of a standard cone of incense. This is done on a heat proof surface such as a censer, atop sand in your cauldron, or on a ceramic or metal altar tile or paten[9]. You light the tip of the mound and allow it to burn for a moment, then gently blow out the flame just as you would a cone. A jar of about 20 grams of this type of incense can be found for around $15 to $25.

Single Incense Charcoal

These recipes will help you whip up a professional-style incense for pennies. All you really need is incense charcoal like the one pictured here, and the herbs, resins, or essential oils required for each recipe. Incense charcoal is not the same as the charcoal you use in outdoor barbecue grills (which emits toxic fumes).

An Altar Paten

Incense charcoal usually comes in a roll of ten disks and can be found where quality incense is sold. A roll will cost about $2 to $5, and will make about ten batches of incense using the recipes provided here.

---

9 A paten is a plate, usually metal, used on an altar for offerings or as a work space. An ornate version is pictured here.

The incense charcoal used in these recipes must be the self-lighting variety. There are many brands available, and I've used Three Kings, Red Ruby, Charcoal Master, Havana, Kwik-Lite, and Swift-Lite successfully. These charcoal disks are about 33mm – 44 mm (around 1½ inch) in diameter.

How to Make Incense Powders

You Will Need

A mortar and pestle (or coffee grinder) and a jar or tin for your finished incense. Don't forget the labels!

Instructions for all Incense Powder Recipes

Working in small batches, grind each ingredient into a powder using your mortar and pestle or coffee grinder. Combine all the powders until thoroughly blended. If a recipe includes essential oils, grind your incense charcoal first, and blend the oils into the powdered charcoal before adding it to the remaining ingredients. **All measurements are for ground or powdered ingredients.**

Powdered Woods & Spices

It is difficult to powder wood at home so you may wish to purchase it already ground. Powdered cedar, cinnamon, and sandalwood are especially useful to have on hand. Ground cloves are also easier to work with than pulverizing whole cloves, and the same goes for allspice. Use white sandalwood powder (*Santalum album)* or Australian sandalwood (*Santalum spicatum*) rather than red sandalwood powder (Pterocarpus santalinus) for these recipes. If you are on a tight budget, substitute pine powder.

There has been concern over the endangerment of sandalwood for the past couple of decades. The primary world supply has historically come out of Mysore, India. However, a policy change in 2002 in several South Indian states allowed additional growers to cultivate sandalwood to prevent endangerment from over-harvesting.

Although sandalwood is still best known to come from India, there are also sustainable plantations in Australia. The Australian Sandalwood Network formed in 2003, and we are finally seeing the long-awaited results of these dedicated growers. Like sandalwood from India, the Australian sandalwood is an excellent incense base.

Purification Incense Powder

This blend is suited to banishing, cleansing, exorcism, clearing, and purification.

Ingredients	Optional Ingredients
1 incense charcoal	1 tsp. Copal and/or Frankincense
¼ cup Rosemary	½ tsp. Sage and/or Cedar

Blessing Incense Powder

This incense is useful for consecrating altar tools, for general ritual use, on Sabbats and Esbats, and to promote peaceful and harmonious energy in your home.

Ingredients	Optional Ingredients
1 incense charcoal	1 T White Copal
¼ cup Sandalwood	1 tsp. Frankincense
½ tsp. Benzoin Resin	½ tsp. Sage
½ tsp. Cinnamon	3 drops Clove Bud essential oil

Prosperity Incense Powder

A money-drawing incense for prosperity rituals and spells.

Ingredients	Optional Ingredients
1 incense charcoal	1 tsp. Patchouli
¼ cup Sandalwood	½ tsp. Violet Flowers
½ tsp. Benzoin Resin	½ tsp. Cloves
½ tsp. Cinnamon	Pinch of Carnation Flowers

Dragon's Blood Incense Powder

A magical catalyst incense used to increase your personal power and add a boost to spells. It is useful for purification and protection, and adapts well to love and lust workings.

Ingredients	
1 incense charcoal	1 tsp. Copal (black preferred)
¼ C Cinnamon	¼ tsp. Clove Bud Essential Oil
1 tsp. Benzoin Resin	2 tsp. Dragon's Blood Resin

Rosemary Incense Powder

This is an excellent blend for cleansing tools and spaces, meditation, study, blessing, and for daily use.

Ingredients	Optional Ingredients
1 incense charcoal	½ C Rosemary Powder

Protection Incense Powder

This incense weaves multiple layers of protection against nightmares, psychic vampires, negative energies, hexes and curses, and other magical, spiritual, or psychic attacks.

Ingredients	
1 incense charcoal	Include a pinch of at least one of the following ingredients. If you have them on hand, add a pinch of all of them.
2 T Sandalwood	
1 T Juniper Leaves/Needles	
1 T Pine Leaves/Needles	Basil, Ginger, Angelica, Agrimony, Elder Flowers, Sage, Black Pepper, Frankincense, Dragon's Blood
1 T Rosemary	
1 Bay Leaf	
½ tsp. Cinnamon	Increase the potency by adding a black tourmaline or obsidian to the jar for storage.
½ tsp. Allspice	
½ tsp. Star Anise	

Third-Eye Opener Incense Powder

This recipe uses mugwort, also known as black sage. Burn this incense when you wish to see spirits, use tarot, scrying, or other forms of divination. It is excellent for dream recall and lucid dreaming, as well as astral travel and out-of-body work.

Ingredients	
1 incense charcoal	1 tsp. Damiana
¼ C Mugwort	1 T Rosemary
1 tsp. Lavender	1 tsp. Juniper Needles and/or Thyme

Love & Romance Incense Powder

Give your romantic encounters a magical boost!

Ingredients	
1 incense charcoal	1 tsp. Cinnamon
¼ C Sandalwood	½ tsp. Lavender Flowers
1 tsp. Benzoin	Pinch of Basil or 1 drop Basil Essential Oil
1 tsp. Rose Petals	3 drops Rose Absolute or undiluted premium rose fragrance oil

Incense Powder Trouble-Shooting

The wide variety of incense charcoal formulations and the unpredictable amount of trace moisture in dried herbs are both factors that may require you to fine-tune your formulas. Use these tips to make adjustments as needed.

If your incense won't stay lit: Make sure all of your ingredients are very dry. Store your incense in a sealed container with a desiccant packet re-used from pill bottles. Try adding and additional ½ of an incense charcoal. Test your new blend and add more charcoal in small increments as necessary.

If your incense flares up, burns too fast, or a flame reappears after you've blown it out: Add more of the first ingredient listed under the charcoal in your recipe. Mix in a teaspoon at a time and test before adding more.

Recipe Trivia:
Using incense charcoal is an easy way to work with potassium nitrate, the chemical that makes these charcoals self-lighting and keeps incense burning. The alchemical symbol for potassium nitrate (also know as nitre or saltpetre) is a circle with a vertical line through the center.

Forming Cones with Incense Powder

Pictured to the right is a Vantine's incense tin from the early 1930s. It came with a metal, cone-shaped tong made of spring steel in the shape of a cone. You would push it into the incense, squeeze to compact the powder,, and release the cone shaped powder into your censer[10].

This inspired the creation of a cone-former made of paper. Cut out a paper circle with a ¼ pie wedge removed as indicated by the dotted lines below. Twist the paper and overlap the edge to form a cone. Larger circles = larger cones.

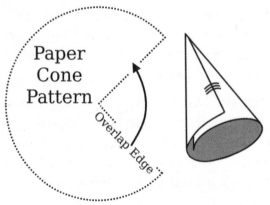

Paper Cone Pattern

Overlap Edge

Hold on the spot marked ≋ while filling.

Hold the edges together on the spot marked with the triple lines. Pack your incense power into the cone gently but firmly. Tip the cone into your censer and gently release your hold on the triple lines.

For a more durable cone former, up-cycle the plastic lid from a yogurt container. Cut off the lip to make the lid flat, and proceed to cut out the ¼ pie wedge and twist as above for the paper version. Plastic's resiliency helps to release the cone.

---

10 Vantine's has a fascinating history involving the Gold Rush, drug mobs, international trade and more. See http://vantines.net

Making Meals Magical

Practical Witches rarely overlook an opportunity to bring a bit of magic into everyday situations. Meal preparation is a good time to incorporate wortcunning into your daily practice. These spice blends correspond to specific magical uses. Add your intent and you have magic sprinkles for meals!

For these recipes, combine all the ingredients together in a large bowl or cauldron. Omit any ingredients that cause you allergies, that you don't like, or that you do not have on hand. Use deosil blending movements while focusing your intent and sending it into the mixture. Store your blends in labeled[11] jars.

Protection Blend

Sprinkle over pizza, eggs, pasta, and other savory dishes. All ingredients are dry, and are the standard ground, powdered, granulated, or chopped leaves found in the spice section of your grocer. This recipe makes about ½ cup.

2 T. Paprika	2 T Chives
2 tsp. Basil	1 tsp. Nettle
3 T Garlic	2 T Parsley
1 tsp. Marjoram	¼ tsp. Sage
¼ tsp. Ginger Root	1 tsp. Rosemary
½ tsp. Cardamom	Pinch each of:
¼ tsp. Turmeric	Cinnamon, Mustard
1 tsp. Black Pepper	Powder, Dill, Cayenne,
1 tsp. Sea Salt (optional)	and Cumin

---

11 Labeling your creations is an important habit to adopt in order to avoid terrible mishaps. That said, don't let labeling your specific spiritual path be too limiting. In my *Practical Witch Talk* podcast, you'll hear me say, "Save your labels for the herb cupboard!"

Love & Friendship Blends

These two blends can be used for either main courses or desserts. Use the Savory & Salty version on eggs, roasted vegetables, pasta, pizza, etc. Sprinkle the Sweets & Desserts blend on top of frosting, cakes, and pastries. For ready-made solutions[12], pumpkin pie spice can be charged with your intention and used in place of the Sweets & Desserts blend.

Savory & Salty	Sweets & Desserts
2 tsp. Rosemary 1 tsp. Basil ½ tsp. Coriander ½ tsp. Thyme ¼ tsp. Catnip Pinch each of: Cumin and Dill	1 T Cinnamon ¼ tsp. Clove 2 tsp. Ginger ½ tsp. Dried Lemon Zest* 1 tsp. Dried Orange Zest* Pinch of Star Anise *Use dried, granulated zests.

Friendship Cookies

An easy recipe to share with friends. Blend the ingredients in the left column in a bowl. Combine the ingredients in the right column in a separate bowl. Combine both bowls and form the dough into walnut size balls, flatten balls slightly onto a greased cookie sheet and bake at 325°F for 10-15 minutes (or until edges are browned and centers are set up). The extra **Sweets & Desserts** blend used here is optional.

¾ C Brown Sugar ¾ C softened Butter or Coconut Oil 3 C Rolled Oats ½ tsp. Salt 1 Large Egg	1 box Spice Cake Mix ¼ C Flour ½ tsp. Sweets & Desserts Blend 1 tsp. Vanilla Extract ⅓ C Apple Juice or Water 1 C Raisins or Dried Cranberries 1 C Nuts or Sunflower Seeds

12 Vanilla is also a wonderful ready-made potion for love and friendship.

Core Practices

Beginners, intermediate, and advanced practitioners all benefit from reviewing the core practices of magic used in Witchcraft. Every time you practice working with energy, you have the opportunity to learn something new.

Box Breathing: Sit or lie down with your back straight. Inhale through your nose to the count of four. Hold for another count of four and then exhale through your mouth to the count of four. Wait four more seconds and then repeat, inhale 4, hold 4, exhale 4, hold 4, etc. Try practicing this breathing technique for five minutes every day, whenever you are stressed, or at the beginning of meditation.

Visualization: Keep your mental powers sharp by regularly visualizing. Listening to audio-books and reading will help you hone your visual skills, along with these exercises.

Exercise 1: In this exercise, you will be visualizing a single color field. Close your eyes and try to visualize just the color red filling all of your inner vision. Think about red and "see" red. This may take some time, but be patient and keep working at it. Try this several times throughout the day and especially before bed until you can easily accomplish this single color visualization.

If you find it difficult to do this visualization, don't get frustrated. Each time you attempt this exercise, you are developing your skills. One day you will find that it is so simple for you to accomplish this visualization that you'll wonder how it was ever so challenging.

Try different colors: Red, Orange, Yellow, Green, Blue, Indigo, Violet. You may find one color is easier to see than others. You may also discover it is easier for you to do this visualization at certain times of the day or night, during different moon phases, or during different personal moods.

Exercise 2: In this exercise, you will be visualizing a single, two-dimensional shape of a solid color. Start by picturing a flat, red circle as if it were printed on a piece of paper. Try other colors: Red, Orange, Yellow, Green, Blue, Indigo, Violet. Change the shape to a square, then try more complex shapes.

Exercise 3: Visualize a sphere or ball. This three-dimensional shape exercise is easier if you can find a simple sphere around your home or at a store. Ping-pong balls, gum-ball machine "super" balls, and other smooth spherical objects work well.

Place the ball in front of you on a table or hold it cupped in your hands. Close your eyes and try to visualize the sphere. Open your eyes occasionally to verify the accuracy of your visualization.

Once you can clearly bring the image of the ball into your mind's eye, change its color. Start with red and continue through orange, yellow, green, blue, indigo, and violet.

Casting Circles:
Practice constructing a quick shield or casting a circle. A circle contains the energy you raise within it until you wish to release it into the universe. It also keeps other energies out of the circle to prevent interference. There are many rituals described in books and online, but the sphere is the core foundation of what you are visualizing and focusing on while performing a circle casting.

Circle Casting 1: Close your eyes and visualize a bubble surrounding you. This bubble extends through everything including the ground (A), and below your feet. You may draw a boundary (B) where your sphere intersects the ground to guide you, and this is often done by covens to assist with precise group visualization. As you become skilled at this visual exercise, or if you are already an experienced practitioner, flex your mental muscles by visualizing the sphere changing colors from swirling violet energy to blue, then green, yellow, orange, and red. For a great protection circle, imagine that your sphere is made of a flexible membrane-like gelatin that you can see through. To someone outside of the circle, visualize it being metallic, like reflective sunglasses. Take this exercise even further by shrinking your sphere down to a small ball that fits in your hand (C) and the expanding it back out to surround you.

Circle Casting 2: Visualize a small sphere of energy in the palm of your hand. Open your perceptions and feel the sphere in your palm. Does it tingle? Is it warm or cold? Does it vibrate? Visualize the sphere growing larger, pushing through you as it grows. See it extend out around you until you are inside of it. It extends down past the ground just like the circle casting on the last page. Next, change the color of your sphere from red to orange, yellow, green, blue, indigo, and violet. Once you've visualized all these colors, see the sphere shrink back down. See and feel it grown smaller until it fits into your hand again.

Storing Energy in Tools: Visualize a sphere in the palm
of your hand and expand it to surround you. Open your eyes (if they aren't already) and see the circle around you. Using your wand or athame, pull the sphere into your ritual tool. Drawn the energy into the tool as if you were vacuuming it up. Now walk deosil around your circle area and push the energy back out of your ritual tool, as if it were water flowing out and forming a bubble around you again. Ritual tools become more powerful over time when you use them consistently for magic.

Shielding: Begin by doing some box breathing. Visualize a
silver cord running from the base of your spine down through

the floor, through the layers of earth, and then anchoring to the earth's core like a magnet. This cord can move freely through material objects but is anchored to the center of the earth and to the base of your spine. As you inhale on the count of four, see energy coming up from the earth along this cord, up your spine and through your chakras, filling your body from head to toe, and then emanating out of the top of your head. Once it exits your physical body it cascades down around you like the branches of a weeping willow tree until it reconnect with the ground. It travels into the core of the earth down and around the outside of your cord as you exhale.

 Breathe in the energy, breathe out the stress and yuck. The earth neutralizes this energy. As you continue breathing and visualizing, you become enveloped inside the cascade of energy flowing back into the earth. When you feel that the energy entering is balanced with the energy exiting, reinforce your visualization of the shield it has created around you.

Journaling & Study: Read as much as you can and keep a journal to record your rituals, thoughts, ideas, recipes, and anything else that comes to mind. This is your book of shadows. It can improve your magic and your mental health.

Words of Power: Use words to carry your energy out into the universe. Words of power are spoken with intent and a commanding tone. You are making a statement that something is already so. Chanting your words of power, repeating them for a spell or ritual, and trying various pitches will help you learn to strike just the right chord for manifestation. You'll know it when you get it, just keep practicing.

Words of power often rhyme for several reasons. Rhymes are much easier to remember and reduce the need to read from your book of shadows. In this way you can focus on your will and intent instead of reading. It also causes a certain familiarity and resonance in the subconscious that adds extra energy to your words.

As a final note, remember that words have power and your inner dialog can affect your mental state. Don't berate yourself aloud or internally. That voice in your head that says you are fat, ugly, stupid, or some other derogatory label isn't you. It was probably put there by other people and you don't need to hold onto that negativity. Be kind to yourself.

Understand Basic Magical Principles:
Sir James George Frazer coined the term "sympathetic magic" in *The Golden Bough* in 1889. Sympathetic magic is used to some degree in every faith and culture worldwide. Throughout history, people have built a variety of techniques based on the two main principles of sympathetic magic. Similar to the laws of physics, these principles are regarded as the basic foundation on which we build our rituals and spells. Once you understand these two principles, you can craft a style of magic that resonates with you better than spells created by others. The first principle is the **Law of Similarities** and the second is the **Law of Contagion**.

Law of Similarities: This is the principle of "like attracts like". Similarities can be in the form of imitation such as a fetish or poppet made to resemble the target of a spell, or a photo being used as a focus for a spell. Similarities may also be drawn through correspondences. When we use plants, stones, and other items that are associated with certain traits we are using the Law of Similarity through correspondences.

The Doctrine of Signatures was a concept used for centuries to determine the correspondence of an item with a trait. An item such as a walnut looks similar to the human brain. The Doctrine of Signatures tells us that walnuts then must be good for the brain. This doctrine assumed that Mother Nature labeled items for our use. The practice has been surprisingly successful, leading us to use foxglove's heart-shaped leaves to indicate its usefulness for the heart. To this day, digitalis (a primary chemical found in foxglove) is used as a heart medicine[13].

Often a correspondence of a trait with a color, herb, or crystal will develop through repeated use by a culture. In Western occultism, the color green is associated with growth and money. We see the lush green abundance of the forests and grasslands and associate the color with growth, and U.S. dollars are green in color. However, in China and Japan, red is associated with abundance, prosperity, and vitality in a way Western occultists associate the color green. Red envelopes containing money are exchanged at the Chinese New Year.

Law of Contagion: This is the principle that two things that have been in contact with each other maintain a magical link as the essence of each is imbued into the other. Think of it like the transfer of molecules when two people or things come into contact, or the transfer of fingerprints left on items.

The magical link that remains between two things can only be severed through time or intent such as a cleansing, banishing, or consecration ritual. This is why the ritual tools used on the Witch's altar are cleansed and consecrated before their first use. The cleansing severs previous magical links, and the consecration sets the tool aside as dedicated to the Witch's intent to prevent it from becoming re-contaminated.

In sympathetic magical practice, the Law of Contagion is often combined with the Law of Similarity such as with the use of a poppet. A doll might be fashioned to look similar to the target of a spell (Similarity). Hair from the target might be used as the poppet's hair, or pieces of fabric from a target's clothing might be used as stuffing or to make clothes for the poppet (Contagion).

Imagine someone has asked you to send healing energy to them after a knee replacement surgery. A poppet could be

---

13 On that note, foxglove is very toxic and should not be consumed. The practice of the Doctrine of Signatures was fraught with the potential for error and has been abandoned in modern medicine and herbalism.

stuffed with a mixture of herbs corresponding to healing such as rosemary, lavender, and mint. You could add healing stones such as moss agate and bloodstone. The hair could be donated from the person requesting the healing (the spell's target) and while focusing your intent you can channel healing energy with pinpoint accuracy to send healing energy to the person's knee through a pin.

Understanding Magic & Probabilities: Magic does not make things manifest without support from you in the mundane world. What magic **will** do is increase the probability that things will manifest the way you desire. A spell to get a job rarely works without putting in some applications.

Gratitude: Regularly performing a gratitude ritual is highly recommended and one has been included in this almanac.

Cleansing, Charging, Blessing, and Consecration: These are important basic skills that are best understood through example. The section on the next page demonstrates the nuances of cleansing, consecrating, and charging with two sample rituals for creating a magical tool and a charged stone.

Do You Need Tools?
There are many Witches who will tell you that you don't need tools, and they're right, mostly. You can perform magic with nothing other than your mind, will, desire, and intent. You can also twist a screw into wood with your hands but a screwdriver makes it a hell of a lot easier! I used to be the purist who preached from the soapbox about how tools were just commercialization of our spirituality. But, after 35+ years of practice I am firmly in the "tools are cool" camp. You don't have to collect a huge array of trinkets, but a few stones, crystals, maybe a cauldron and an athame or wand can be very useful to focus your energy. If you feel drawn to a crystal or tool, try it out! Did you find a stick you really like on your walk? Make it your wand!

The Witch's Tools Paradox

While studying some Witchcraft traditions, you may come across instructions for creating your magical altar tools. These instructions tell you to use your consecrated athame to inscribe or direct power into the tools you are creating. The paradox is, how do you create a consecrated athame or tool if you don't already have a consecrated athame?

To consecrate something, it means that you are setting it apart from the mundane and making it sacred. Before something is consecrated, it is spiritually cleansed. Traditionally, salt is considered pure and is incorporated into cleansing rituals prior to consecration. A common example of this is the making of holy water in the Catholic church. Salt, considered "pure" is blessed with prayers. Water (considered "impure") is prayed over and a little blessed salt is sprinkled into it (making it exorcised/cleansed), and it is then sanctified (made holy, consecrated) with more prayers.

Cleansing

Cleansing is a core practice of Witchcraft. Crystals, stones, and tools can be cleansed in moonlight, sunlight, censed[14] in the smoke of sacred herbs, or submerged in running water. No matter what technique is used, visualization and intent play key roles. While cleansing an item, imbue it with the intent of removing all other energies. Visualize white (or whatever color you like) energy flowing through you and into the item. Cleansing creates somewhat of an energy vacuum and should be followed-up with charging, blessing, or consecration.

---

14 Cense and censing means *to infuse with smoke* or *to perfume with burning incense*. The term has been in use since the 14th century. Although "smudging" is frequently misused to mean the same thing, smudging is part of several Indigenous cultures and is closed to those who are not part of those cultures. Smoke-cleansing is a type of censing.

Charging & Consecration

When you "charge" an item, you program it with a specific intent, giving it a particular purpose or duties. You might charge a stone for protection or luck, while you would consecrate your altar tools for general magical and sacred uses. The following ritual for making a magical wand or athame and a charging a crystal for protection clarifies cleansing and consecration.

Cleansing & Consecrating a Wand or Athame

Cleansing: Cast a circle and place the tool (wand or athame) in front of you along with a bowl of water (you may use your moon water), a small dish of salt, incense, and a candle.

> **Witch's Blessed Water:** Take three small pinches of salt and sprinkle it into the water while focusing your intent. You might say words of power you have designed or chant:
>
> *"Three times three, I purify thee."*
>
> This magically purifies the water. Next, bless the water to consecrate it by focusing on the intent for which the water will be used and speaking words of power you have designed or:
>
> *"Water pure and blessed be,*
> *as is my will, so mote it be"*

Draw energy up from the earth and through your body. Feel energy moving upwards along your spine and through your chakras. Move the energy down your arms and into the tool. You can pick up the tool, touch it, or simply look at it to aid the flow of energy. Visualize the tool glowing with energy. Focus your intent on removing all previous energies the tool may contain. Close your eyes and visualize the tool down to its most minute detail. You can open your eyes occasionally to verify details. Continue visualizing until you can see it clearly in your visualization. Your tool is now cleansed and ready for consecration to dedicate it to your magical use.

Consecrating: Witches prefer to consecrate altar tools with the four classical elements; air, fire, water, and earth. When you blessed the water, you purified it with salt which corresponds to the earth element. Sprinkle the water over the tool while chanting:

"Water and earth, I give you rebirth"

Lightly pass the wand or athame through the candle flame and then the incense smoke while chanting:

"Air and fire, work my desire."

Your tool is now consecrated to the purpose of your magical and spiritual practice. It has an ethereal body that is present on other planes of existence. You reinforced this ethereal body during the visualization you did right before the consecration. Consecrated tools should be kept in a safe location where they will not be picked up or handled by others. It isn't going to ruin them, but it prevents the need to cleanse them repeatedly. With that in mind, remember that it is important to never touch the tools and jewelry belonging to other practitioners without their express permission. It may also be wise to store ritual blades away from children and visitors who may not understand their purpose.

Every time you use a ritual tool it grows in power as does your ability to work with it. Include your ritual tools on your altar for Sabbats and Esbats, even if you aren't specifically using them during rituals and festivities. If you do a daily meditation or gratitude ritual, consider doing so in front of an altar where you store your tools.

Charging a Stone for Protection

Now that you have a consecrated tool, you can use it to help focus and direct your energy when charging objects. Select an object you wish to carry for protection. Some stones that work well for this are black tourmaline, black obsidian, tiger eye, and clear quartz.

Cleanse the stone by letting it soak in the bowl of blessed water for a few minutes. You can also expose it to moonlight or sunlight* for an hour to cleanse it prior to your ritual. Focus your energy with the same visualization as you used to consecrate your tool. Hold your wand or athame and draw energy up from the earth, through the tool, and into the stone. Notice how the tool really helps channel your power! While visualizing and projecting your energy, you may wish to say words of power or vocalize an affirmation such as:

"Three time three I charge thee,
to protect from harm sent to me."

* Caution:

The color of some stones such as amethyst, rose quartz, ruby, and aventurine may fade in sunlight. Avoid leaving these exposed to sunlight for long periods of time. They can also be cleansed in running water, moonlight, or by censing. Minerals like calcite and selenite may be damaged by water and are best cleansed by censing, sunlight, and moonlight.

Clear quartz gets a powerful charge from sunlight, but use caution when sunning spheres, eggs, and other quartz with curved shapes as these are especially good at magnifying sunlight and starting fires.

Houseplants for Magic & Health

Houseplants improve our moods, make us feel more relaxed, and have been shown by NASA to remove toxins from our environment. Cohabitation with plants has many magical and spiritual benefits as well. When you are stuck indoors or live in an urban setting, living with houseplants can help you stay connected to the earth. This list will help you select the potted roommate that is magically right for you.

Please Note: If you have pets or young children, remember that many houseplants are toxic. Use hanging planters to keep them out of reach, or select specific varieties noted as ***pet safe***. Of course even non-toxic plants may pose a choking hazard, and may induce vomiting in pets. Pay close attention to binomials (botanical or scientific names) when choosing a pet safe option. Do your own research[15] and talk with your vet or medical pro to be certain. If you notice anyone consuming these plants (even large quantities of those marked ***pet safe***), or if you notice symptoms of dermatitis or illness after handling plants, call the Poison Control help line at 800- 222-1222.

African Violets: prosperity, love, beauty

Air Plants: communication, divination, anti-nightmare, creativity, inspiration

Bamboo: love, peace, longevity, harmony, wealth *Bambusa multiplex* (a type of Bamboo) and *Phyllostachys aurea* (Golden Bamboo) are ***pet safe***

Chrysanthemum: (Florist's Daisy, Garden Mum), longevity, energy, rejuvenation, protection from negative spirits and hexes, ancestral altars, warding, blessing incense, *Chrysanthemum morifolium*, removes benzene, formaldehyde, trichloroethylene, xylene, toluene, and ammonia

Cyclamen: joy, happiness, love, fertility, sacred to Hecate

---

15 University of California, Davis, has a great PDF of *Safe and Poisonous Garden Plants* to get you started
    https://ucanr.edu/sites/poisonous_safe_plants/files/154528.pdf

English Ivy: *Hedera helix*, protection, binding, fertility, abundance. Removes benzene, formaldehyde, tricholorethylene, xylene, and toluene from the environment.

Fern: protection, blending-in, shielding

>**Kimberley Queen Fern**, *Nephrolepis obliterata*, is a ***pet safe*** fern that removes formaldehyde, xylene, and toluene from the environment.
>**Boston Fern**, *Nephrolepis exaltata*, is also ***pet safe***

Ficus/Fig: *Ficus benjamina* (weeping fig), protection, happiness, removes formaldehyde, xylene, and toluene

Lemon: love, protection, prosperity, purification, friendship, harmony, happiness, awareness *Grown your own lemon tree from the seeds from inside a grocery store lemon. Using your creativity, you can invent a great spell for prosperity, or grow extra trees and give them away to help bond friendships.*

Norfolk Island Pine: appetite suppressant, affluence, good luck, protection

Orchids: romance, love, passion, eloquence

>**Moth orchid**, *halanopsis*, removes xylene and toluene

Palms: banishing negativity, peace, tranquility

>**Dragon Palm:** or *Dracaena* are magical catalysts that add energy to spells and filter out benzene, formaldehyde, trichloroethylene, xylene, and toluene

>**Broadleaf Lady Palm:** *Rhapis excelsa*, is ***pet safe***

>**Bamboo Palm:** (Parlour Palm) *Chamaedorea elegans*, is ***pet safe*[16]** and removes formaldehyde, xylene, and toluene

---

16 The ASPCA has a Poison Control Center Number: 888-426-4435 and a *Toxic and Non-Toxic Plants List* https://www.aspca.org/pet-care/animal-poison-control/toxic-and-non-toxic-plants

Peace Lilies: harmony, calm, peace. An outstanding plant for removing benzene, formaldehyde, xylene, trichloroethylene, toluene, and ammonia from the environment.

Pothos: *Epipremnum aureum* (formerly Pothos aureus) money, prosperity, abundance. Removes benzene, formaldehyde, xylene, and toluene from the environment.

Spider Plant: *Chlorophytum comosun* protection, warding. Removes xylene, formaldehyde, and toluene. ***pet safe***

Pothos is easily grown from cuttings

Succulents: protection, prosperity, abundance, good luck, friendship, abundance, healing. In addition to these correspondences, certain succulents are especially well suited to specific intentions...

Aloe: healing, fertility

Cacti and Thorned Succulents: protection, warding, prickly spines can be used for poppets[17] and in spells.

Christmas Cactus: *Schlumbergera russelliana* harmony, blessing, friendship, prosperity, ***pet safe***

Hen & Chicks: *Sempervivum tectorum* is ***pet safe***

Jade, String-of-Pearls, Burro's Tail: prosperity, abundance, and luck. Burro's Tail, *Sedum morganianum*, is ***pet safe***

Snake Plant: (Mother in Law's Tongue), *Sansevieria trafasciata*, protection, removes benzene, formaldehyde and tricholoethylene from the environment

---

17 A poppet is a figure or doll fashioned according to the magical Law of Similarity to look like the target of a spell. The Law of Contagion can be employed by incorporating hair or other items from the target.

Zodiac Correspondences

Each sign corresponds to a classical element. After the name of each sign is noted the Quality | Ruler | Symbol

Water Signs

♋ Cancer - Cardinal | Moon | The Crab

♏ Scorpio - Fixed | Pluto/Mars | The Scorpion

♓ Pisces - Mutable | Neptune | The Fish

Water

Fire Signs

♈ Aries - Cardinal | Mars | The Ram

♌ Leo - Fixed | Sun | The Lion

♐ Sagittarius - Mutable | Jupiter | The Archer

Fire

Earth Signs

♉ Taurus - Fixed | Venus | The Bull

♍ Virgo - Mutable | Mercury | The Virgin

♑ Capricorn - Cardinal | Saturn | The Goat

Earth

Air Signs

♊ Gemini - Mutable | Mercury | The Twins

♎ Libra - Cardinal | Venus | The Scales

♒ Aquarius - Fixed | Uranus | The Water Bearer

Air

Potions for Magic & Zodiac Signs

Select any formula that corresponds to your desire and intent. Then, brew up a cup to use as the libation in your spell or ritual. You can also use these formulas as bath teas. Although each tea is recommended for a specific astrological sign, **you can use any of these formulas as desired regardless of your sign**.

All ingredients are dried and cut or chopped to approximately equal sizes. When ordering licorice root, echinacea root, turmeric, cinnamon, and other hard botanicals, it is easier to buy them already chopped into pieces instead of trying to process them at home. Hibiscus is easier to work with if you purchase "cut flowers" rather than whole flowers.

General Instructions:

Combine all ingredients and store in a dark, cool location in a labeled, airtight container. If you do not have one of the ingredients, you can skip it. For hot tea, use 1-2 tsp. brewed for 3 minutes in 8 ounces of very hot water (210°F+). For iced tea, use 2-3 tsp. of the blend, brew, cool, and pour over ice. Recipes with roots and berries benefit from an extra minute or two of steeping. Re-brew the used botanicals for a second cup to get every last drop of the benefits.

Formulation Notes:

These formulas use botanicals when they 1) are traditionally associated with the corresponding sign 2) also correspond to studies in which they have shown promise for certain ailments, 3) when they are generally regarded as safe.

The magical correspondences of each botanical is considered, and then the synergistic combination of the botanicals is analyzed to provide you with the overall magical uses for each blend.

Caution:

You may have never consumed some of the ingredients in these formulas. Because of this, it is recommended that you proceed slowly, taking your first sip and waiting an hour to make sure you don't have an immediate allergic reaction. Do not use these formulas if you are pregnant or nursing. Omit Black Cohosh (Black Snakeroot) from a recipe if you are sensitive to aspirin as this botanical contains salicylic acids.

This almanac is not intended as a substitute for the medical advice of a qualified health care professional. Consult a physician in matters relating to health. This information is not intended to diagnose, treat, cure, or prevent any condition or disease.

Aries

Fuel your fire with this tea. You might also get extra energy by eating pumpkin seeds regularly.

Dream Work, Meditation, Mild Vermifuge
2 T. Chamomile, 2 T. Lemon Balm,
2 tsp. Cinnamon Chips, 1 T. Mugwort.

Taurus

Keep your tummy and intestines happy while boosting your earthy energy.

Purification, Protection, Success
2 T. Chamomile, 1 T. Calendula Flowers,
1 tsp. Marshmallow Leaves, 1 tsp. Licorice Root Chips
1 tsp. Slippery Elm, 1tsp. Marjoram, 1 tsp. Cramp Bark
1 tsp. Cat's Claw (Uncaria Tomentosa)

Gemini

Stay in harmony with this herbal blend. This is especially effective if you substitute the tea for your regular alcoholic or caffeinated beverage.

Divination, Dreams, Ancestral Work, Meditation
1 T. Milk Thistle Flowers, 2 T. Dandelion Leaves
2 T. Peppermint, 1 T. Passion Flower, 2 tsp. Damiana
1 tsp. Basil, 1 tsp. Scullcap

Cancer

Keep your water flowing by eating apples regularly and try this tea before large meals. This blend may help soothe intestinal inflammation.

Luck, Un-Crossing, Anti-Hex, Protection, Success
2 T. Chamomile, 1 T. Mullein, 1 T. Lemon Balm, 1 T. Scullcap
2 tsp. Licorice Root, 1 tsp. Thyme.

Leo

Garlic and ginseng will keep your lion's roar strong, and this tea will keep your fire from burning out. This is a general health and immune boosting formula.

Power, Strength, Prosperity, Protection
1 T. Echinacea Root Chips, 1 T. Dried Elderberries
1 T. Dried Ginger Root Chips, 1 T. Lemon Balm
1 T. Nettle Leaves, 1 T. Hibiscus Chopped
1 tsp. Licorice Root Chips, 1 tsp. Turmeric Root Chips.

Virgo

Stay connected to the earth while soothing your tummy (and preventing nausea) with this easy blend. Steep extra long for more ginger heat.

Transformation, Love, Lust, Prosperity
Eloquence, Confidence, Self-Assertion
2 T. Ginger Root Chips, 2 T. Peppermint Leaves
1 T. Fennel Seeds.

Libra

Keep your scales balanced with a strong foundation. Calcium, Magnesium, and Vitamin D are your friends. This great tea may boost your strength and supply trace minerals for bone health. If you make this tea with green tea, try adding 1 T. Peppermint Leaves and serve iced.

Protection, Hex-Reversal, Un-Crossing
Courage, Vitality, Virility, Love
2 T Rooibos (or Green Tea), 1 T. Nettle Leaves
1 T. Black Cohosh (a.k.a. Black Snake Root)
1 T. Dandelion Leaves, 1 T. Horsetail, 1 T. Red Clover
1 T. Alfalfa, 1 T. Lemongrass

Scorpio

Keep the sting in your tail from biting you in the ass. This herbal tea blend is good for general inflammation and colon health, and you can use a strong infusion in a sitz bath.

Protection, Prosperity, Luck,
Exorcism, Purification
2 T. Turmeric Root Chips, 1 T. Calendula Flowers
1 T. Plantain Leaves, 2 tsp. Licorice Root Chips

Sagittarius

Balance your fire and keep your aim on target with this tea blend. Sagittarians may also benefit from the Libra tea.

Prosperity, Focus, Protection

2 T. Peppermint, 1 T. Lemongrass1 T. Nettle Leaves
1 T. Dandelion Leaves, 1 T. Horsetail, 1 T. Red Clover

Capricorn

Stay focused and avoid capriciousness with this grounding tea. Capricorns may also benefit from the Leo general health and immunity tea.

Prosperity, Luck, Abundance, Wisdom, Decision Making

1 T. Dried Elderberries, 1 T. Lemon Verbena, 1 T. Lemon Balm
2 T. Dried Ginger Root Chips, 2 tsp. Turmeric Root Chips
1 tsp. Licorice Root Chips

Aquarius

Keep your air energy flowing with this tea that is also helpful for reducing inflammation and improved respiration and chest health.

Purification, Blessing, Clarity

2 T. Hibiscus Flowers (cut), 2 tsp. Turmeric Root Chips
2 tsp. Holy Basil, 1 tsp. Alfalfa, 1 tsp. Licorice Root Chips.

Pisces

Boost your assertiveness, confidence, and fortitude with this heart-healthy tea.

Positive Energy, Good Vibes, Divination Compassion, Confidence

1 T. Hawthorn Berries, 1 T. Dried Pomegranate Arils
1 T. Hibiscus Flowers (cut), 1 T. Oregon Grape Root Chips
1 tsp. Black Cohosh (Black Snakeroot).

Working With Moon Phases

There are many approaches to working with lunar energy, and your experiences, tradition, and training may help you determine what works best for you. Social media is rife with memes and info-graphics about working with moon phases in magic, and many of them contradict each other. To clarify the matter in a practical way, the next two pages cover the primary approaches to moon phase magic. In the end, you must use the approach that feels right to you for your personal practice.

A reproduction of an early esoteric grimoire print with calendar engravings. This example is from a magical almanac dating from c. 1619-1620 and is entitled "Calendarium Naturale Magicum Perpetuum". The elemental associations with the seasons are noted in Latin: Aer=Air, Ignis=Fire, Terra=Earth, Aqva (aqua)=Water.

Eight Phases Approach to Moon Magic

The energy cycles we experience as the year passes are similar to the energy cycles we experience during the phases of the moon. Each phase includes a corresponding Sabbat to give you a sense of the energy each moon phase entails.

	New: Beginnings and fresh starts. Sow the seeds of new projects, set intentions, objectives and goals. *Sabbat: Winter Solstice*
	Crescent: Commit to intent, initiative, driving forward toward accomplishment, visualization and taking action. *Sabbat: Imbolc*
	1st Quarter: Manifesting, increased growth, affirmations, trust, effort, will, action. *Sabbat: Vernal (Spring) Equinox*
	Waxing Gibbous: Hone, refine, and perfect your intentions or approach, observe, re-affirm, fine-tuned actions. *Sabbat: Beltane*
	Full: Receive, celebrate, objectivity, clarity, illumination, gratitude, collaboration. *Sabbat: Midsummer, Summer Solstice*
	Waning Gibbous or Disseminating: Gratitude, sharing, reassess intent, culmination. *Sabbat: Lughnasadh, Lammas*
	3rd or Last Quarter: Understanding Banishing, reducing, declining, composting, releasing. *Sabbat: Autumnal (Fall) Equinox*
	Balsamic: Inner reflection, rest, preparation, further shedding of the old to make way for the new. Dark moon time. *Sabbat: Samhain*

Spell-Caster Approach to the Eight Phases

New: Deconstruction magic, banishing, ridding, divination, reflection.	**Full:** All types of magic and divination, combination drawing/banishing spells.
Crescent: Drawing and attraction magic, success, love, money, luck, friendship.	**Waning Gibbous or Disseminating:** Reversals, unbinding, releasing.
1st Quarter: Growth, strength, divination, motivation, encouragement.	**3rd or Last Quarter:** Banishing, releasing, eliminating bad habits, reversals, unbinding.
Waxing Gibbous: Drawing and attraction, success, health, increase.	**Balsamic:** Balance, divination, reflection, recovery, meditation.

Four Phase Approach

This practical approach is effective and easy to remember.

●	**New:** Resting, releasing, banishing, repelling, new beginnings, reversal magic, unbinding.
◐	**Waxing:** Attraction, setting intentions, manifesting, planning, planting, developing, drawing, attraction.
○	**Full:** Celebration, harvest, gratitude, meditation, devotion, protection, all types of magic and divination.
◑	**Waning:** Clearing, cleansing, releasing intentions that were not meant to manifest at this time, re-evaluation, reversals, banishing.

Moon Water, Beyond the Basics

Making moon water has become very popular and there are instructions for how to make it in many books and online. However, I've come across a lot of questions about it while working at a local metaphysical shop and interacting with my students at WitchAcademy.org. This article covers some of the finer points of moon water creation.

What is Moon Water?

Moon water is water that has been charged by the energy of the moon. Usually this is done during the full moon, but you can utilize the energies of any moon phase to charge your water.

What is Moon Water Used For?

Moon water can be used to cleanse stones and altar tools. You can put it in a spray bottle with a little lemon juice for household cleansing and blessing. Use it to water your plants, make tea and extracts, or use it as a ritual libation. Use it for the traditional dish of blessed water on your altar. Add it to lustral baths[18], or if you don't have a bathtub you can pour moon water over your head as a final energy rinse. Your moon water will give your intentions an extra boost of energy and help you with any magical workings.

How Do I Make Moon Water?

Fill a bowl, bottle, or jar with potable[19] water. You can also use dew you've collected off of plants with a sponge, spring water, or rain water. It is important to use potable water if your moon water will be consumed. Remember to prepare and store your moon water in glass or food-safe

---

18 A lustral bath is ritual bathing for purification before rituals.
19 Potable means suitable or safe for drinking.

containers. You can find lovely bottles for this at a thrift stores and metaphysical shops, and even decorate them if you wish.

For full and waxing moon water, place the container of water outside after sunset where it will be exposed to direct moonlight. You might choose to say words of power and focus your intention when you set it out. Allow it to absorb the moon's energy for an hour or more, and remember to bring it back indoors before sunrise. For new and waning moon water, place your container out after sunrise[20] and continue as for full moon water, bringing it indoors before sunset.

Can I Add to Moon Water I've Already Made?

Maybe you have some moon water left from last month and you want to add more water to the bottle and re-charge it under tonight's full moon. There are a few things to consider when doing this. Even when you prepare your moon water with water that is safe for drinking, it contains traces of molds, bacteria, protozoa, and other critters that can multiply over time and cause health problems if the water is consumed. An open bowl of water will collect even more critters as opposed to a capped bottle. You may wish to preserve your moon water as suggested below or avoid drinking it.

Do I Need to Protect Full Moon Water From Sunlight?

Usually, exposure of moon water to sunlight is discouraged. However, sunlight isn't going to erase your intentions or the lunar energy already imbued into the water. A little sunlight will alter the energy of full and waxing moon water only **very slightly**. Maybe you put your moon water out with great intentions of bringing it inside, only to fall asleep and

---

20 The moon is overhead in the daytime during a new moon.

discover it waiting for you in the morning. That's okay, relax, it isn't ruined! It spent the whole night with the moon and you set your intentions into it. Use it as normal and set a timer or alarm to remind yourself to bring it in next time.

Do I Need to Preserve Moon Water?

If you are using moon water within a few days, you probably don't need to preserve it. Remember those critters that live in your water? You don't want them to multiply excessively and set up a whole civilization in your moon water. If you want to store moon water for extended periods of time add a pinch of sea salt to keep it a little safer. After adding salt, you probably shouldn't consume it or use it to water plants (salt is damaging to plants).

You may wish to preserve some moon water, such as lunar eclipse water, for several months or years. This unique water is charged for the entire duration of a lunar eclipse[21] and contains energy similar to all of the moon's phases. To preserve this water, add a pinch of sea salt and 10% food-grade ethyl alcohol. Use the *Apothecary Alligation Method* to determine the amount of alcohol you need based on the liquor you have on hand.

What if I Don't Want to Use Alcohol?

When you want to preserve your moon water without the use of alcohol, you can use an acid to discourage the growth of dangerous microbes. For every 8 ounces of moon water add ½ teaspoon of citric acid or 2 teaspoon of vinegar. Citric acid is inexpensive and easily obtained online, just be sure the type you are getting is food-grade. A pinch of salt will also help prevent microbial growth.

---

21 See your weekly planner pages for the peak times of eclipses. Set your
    water out an hour prior to peak and bring it in before sunrise.

Can I Mix New Moon and Full Moon Water?

Certainly! You can practice your magic any way you like! If you are intuitively drawn to combining your new moon water with your full moon water, then do so. The energy of this combined water tends to be very balancing.

Can I add Stones to My Moon Water for Elixirs?

Yes, of course, with some caveats. Certain stones such as galena and malachite contain toxins that can leech into water, making the moon water potentially toxic. Selenite and calcite can be damaged by prolonged contact with water. Stick with quartz crystals, amethyst, citrine, aventurine, moonstone, garnet, ruby, sapphire, aquamarine, and emerald.

Tinctures, Moon Water, and Hand Sanitizer

Preservation When you wish to store tinctures or moon water for several weeks, use the *Apothecary Alligation Method* to add 10% or more alcohol. When you are especially concerned about preservation (such as when you are giving tinctures as gifts), use a hydrometer to verify the alcohol content. If you make tinctures, mead, kombucha, wine, beer, or ale at home, you may already have a hydrometer. If not, this simple tool can be purchased for under $20 online or at brew supply shops.

Making Tinctures When extracting alcohol-soluble components from botanicals, an 80% alcohol solution is suggested for fresh herbs and at least 40% alcohol for dried plants.

Hand Sanitizer Hand sanitizer can be made by mixing alcohol with aloe vera gel and should be at least 65% alcohol to effectively kill bacteria. For an extra anti-microbial boost – add a drop each of clove bud essential oil, oregano essential oil, and thyme essential oil for every 10 ounces of sanitizer,. If you don't have all three, just add the ones you do have.

Apothecary Alligation Method

This magic square technique is a secret trick that is widely used by apothecaries and pharmacists. Referred to in pharmacy as the Alligation Alternate Method, it is a simple way to calculate the number of parts needed to prepare a solution of the desired strength. **Don't be scared off by the math**, this is crazy simple to understand if you give it a few minutes to sink in. Do yourself a huge favor and study this until you are confident that you can calculate a 10% solution. You'll feel like a genius and the information will serve you in the most unexpected ways throughout your life.

This method uses parts by volume[22]. First you'll need a magic square. The only boxes you'll use are the ones that are not shaded. Take a look below at the basic magic square we'll use to find out how much alcohol you need to mix with your moon water to get a 10% alcohol solution.

percent alcohol in solution **A**		
	percent alcohol you want **X**	
percent alcohol in solution **B**		

You'll fill out information for **A**, **X**, and **B**, and then do some simple subtraction. Don't panic, we'll cover all of this.

---

22 Parts are explained in *The Simpler's Method* article.

What Kind of Alcohol do You Have?

The first box in the top row is where you enter the percentage of alcohol your liquor contains. Stay on the safe side by using food-grade ethyl alcohol. The easiest way to get this is at your local liquor store. Rubbing alcohol from the pharmacy is isopropyl alcohol and should <u>never</u> be consumed! If the alcohol percentage is not listed on your liquor label, find the proof mark and divide by 2.

Proof to Alcohol Percent Examples:
40 Proof Vodka ÷2 = 20% alcohol
100 Proof Dulce Vida Tequila ÷2 = 50% alcohol
190 Proof Everclear or ClearGem ÷ 2 = 95% alcohol
Overproof Rum (like Bacardi 151) 151 ÷ 2 = 75.5% alcohol

The first box in the top row of your magic square is for alcohol, the second row is for the percentage you want to get, and the first box in the bottom row is for the alcohol in your second solution, in this case moon water. We are going to say that you have 40 proof vodka. Since that is 20% alcohol, we put a **20** in the first box as shown below. For moon water, we want 10% alcohol so we enter a **10** the middle box. The first box in the last row is for the alcohol in your second solution, in this case your moon water with 0% alcohol. So that's easy, just enter a **0** in that box. Only two boxes left, you're doing great!

20 the percent alcohol in my vodka **A**		
	10 percent alcohol you **want** to preserve moon water **X**	
0 percent alcohol in moon water **B**		

Moving diagonally from the top left to the bottom right, subtract X from A. For example 20 (A) – 10 (X) = 10.

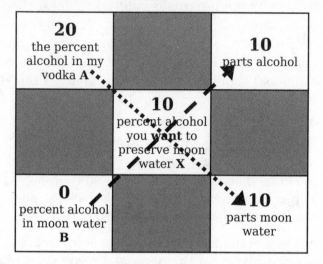

Now using the numbers in the diagonal from the bottom left to the top right, subtract X from B. In this instance, 10 (X) – 0 (B) = 10. Now you know that for every 10 parts of moon water, you need 10 parts of vodka. If your parts are ounces, you'll add 10 oz vodka to 10 oz moon water. Let's do it again, but with an 80 proof (40%) rum.

40 the percent alcohol in 80 proof rum **A**		10 parts alcohol
	10 percent alcohol I want to preserve moon water **X**	
0 percent alcohol moon water **B**		30 parts moon water

A-X=30 (bottom right box), **X-B=10** (top right box). For every 30 ounces or parts of moon water you have, you'll need 10 ounces or parts of rum.

The Baneful Herbs

There has been a recent trend for Witches to dabble with the 'dark herbs'. We regularly use rosemary, thyme, cinnamon, and other plants in food. However, please keep in mind that some plant allies are highly toxic and should not be ingested under any circumstance. Even when there are historical accounts of their consumption, use in smoking mixtures, or inclusion in flying ointments, that does not mean that the 'dark herbs' should be imbibed any more than mercury should be used as a cure for typhoid fever[23].

The 'dark herbs' of old northern Europe such as henbane, wolf's bane, mandrake, datura, and belladonna are wonderful to cultivate for their beauty and magical properties. If you choose to have a poison garden, be sure to keep pets and children away, and post notices to let people know that the plants are toxic. It is difficult to grow these plants safely in urban areas because you never know who might accidentally be poisoned. Please be extra cautious if you live in a populated area.

These plants can safely be used in spell jars, but do not attempt to smoke or consume these plants, Use gloves when handling them and practice careful storage, labeling, and cleanup procedures. Many of these plants have cumulative toxins that damage internal organs. They will harm you even if you cannot immediately tell that they have done so. If the Witches of the past had the abundant access that we do to safer anesthetics and entheogenic plants and fungi, they most certainly would have used them instead. **They learned these lessons the hard way. Honor their memory by respecting the wisdom gained from these Witches, midwives, and shamans of the past by not consuming these plants.**

---

23 Yes, mercury was used to treat typhoid fever, and this was likely the cause of Louisa May Alcott's demise.

The Nightshade (Solanaceae) Family

Atropa Belladonna

Belladonna (Deadly Nightshade) - *Atropa belladonna* is one of the most toxic plants known. With her chemical cocktail of atropine, scopolamine and hyoscyamine you are lucky if you get away with convulsions and vomiting. She is a heart-stopper, literally, and generally messes up your entire nervous system.

Datura - *Datura spp.* can *seem* safe a dozen time, until she isn't. She either stops your breathing or your heart, or both. When she doesn't do this immediately, you just got temporarily lucky as she contains persist cumulative toxins that can damage organs and build up in your body. At best you can expect vomiting, fever, nausea, heart racing, visual disturbances, and general unpleasantness.

Henbane – *Hyoscyamus niger* is another ruthless mistress. Like her sisters in this plant family she contains hyoscyamine, scopolamine, and other tropane alkaloids. This toxic brew leads to vomiting, convulsions, and heart failure more often than it leads to any magic.

Mandrake

European Mandrake – *Mandragora officinarum* and *M. autumnalis* takes your breath away as you die from asphyxiation. Use the root as a poppet or talisman and avoid ingesting the highly biologically active brew of alkaloids (tropane, d atropine, hyoscyamine, scopolamine [hyoscine], scopine, cuscohygrine, apoatropine, and many more) all of which kill you in some of the most horrible ways imaginable.

Other Plants to Use With Caution

Monkshood, (Wolf's-Bane) - *Aconitum spp.* contains large amounts of the highly toxic aconitine and related alkaloids that will introduce you to death quickly. Burning and tingling turn into vomiting and diarrhea. After an hour or so of this torture, your heart just gives up the fight.

Castor – *Ricinus communis* is one of the most toxic common plants around and, holy hand basket what can I say about this to discourage you from using it? It kills. That's it. Just dead. The seeds ("beans") are a powerful source of ricin, a toxin that ingested even in small quantities is relentlessly deadly. Just a few of these lovely magic beans will send you cruising the river Styx, and for children the trip takes even fewer beans. Nausea and diarrhea can last up to a week as the poison works its evil on your insides in a slow and miserable end of life. Stick to castor oil if you wish to use the plant's energies and stay away from the pretty seeds. Castor oil is safe and makes a wonderful addition to homemade lye soap.

To mark your poison plants, you can make plant markers that look like tombstones!

Spell to Find Witchy Friends

Looking for Witchy friends? Someone to hang with? This spell will help you attract like-minded people. Like all magic, it will *increase the probability* that your path will cross with the right individuals. You must follow-up this spell by actually putting yourself out there into the mundane world. Join a group, attend real life or virtual events, go to metaphysical bookstores, etc. Looking for something to do with your new friend? Invite them over to make Friendship Cookies (recipe included in your almanac), give them a lemon tree you grew from seed, or propagate succulents together to help cement the friendship.

You Will Need

Something that Represents You – Select a symbol that represents you or your spiritual path. This might be a pentacle or pendant, a sigil drawn on paper, or some of your hair or nails.

A Small Bottle or Spell Jar – A small glass jar that will hold all of the other ingredients except the candle. Check that the mouth of the jar is large enough to fit the aventurine stone.

One Pink Candle   **1 tsp. Dried Lemon Peel**

Aventurine Stone   **1 tsp. Catnip**

3 Apple Seeds   **3 Drops Vanilla Extract**

Cinnamon or Sandalwood Incense *(optional)*

　　　Prepare yourself for magic as you normally would, relaxing, practicing box breathing, or whatever your practice includes. Light the incense to get things going. If you anoint your candles for spells, do so now. Patchouli, rose, jasmine, or sandalwood oils work well for this spell. Place the pink candle in front of you and light it while saying words of power of your creation or:

> *My heart and spirit call to you,*
> *Come to me, new friends true.*

If you are burning incense, hold the open bottle over it to fill it with smoke. Use your words of power or say:

> *My mind yearns for company,*
> *with whom to talk comfortably.*

Add the apple seeds, catnip, lemon peel, and drops of vanilla extract while saying:

> *Our paths will cross and you will see,*
> *the familiar spirit inside of me.*

Add the aventurine and say:

> *New friends who are meant to be,*
> *will quickly find their way to me.*

Cap the bottle (and seal it with the wax of your pink candle if you like). Hold the bottle in your hands while gazing on the candle and focusing your will and intent. When you are satisfied that you have clearly projected your intent, finish with words of power such as: *This is my will, so mote it be!*

Allow the candle to finish burning out. Keep the spell jar on your altar, under your bed, or somewhere near you.

Mundane World Follow-Up - Right before you go out or connect with others online, hold the bottle and repeat all the words of power you used before. Remember to put yourself out there so your path *can* cross with someone new. Also, be aware of your personal friendship restrictions. Be open to people who may not be your same age, gender, or economic status! Broaden your horizons, and it doesn't hurt to wear something that other Witches can use to help identify you. A printed t-shirt, crystal, pentacle, or other piece of jewelry can help.

Breaking Bonds Ritual

It can be difficult to break away from deep and intense relationships. This is especially true when a magical, psychic, or empathic bond remains. You might hear a song on the radio and it reminds you of your ex, and then a text message from that person pops up on your phone![24] Yikes! When it is time to leave a relationship in your past, breaking the energy bonds can free you. **Before you begin, review the relationship and the lessons it brought to you.** When you have processed this as best you can, sever the energy connections with this bond breaking ritual and leave that toxic relationship in your past.

---

24 If you are being stalked or are in danger, contact a crisis resource like the National Domestic Violence Hotline at 1-800-799-SAFE (7233). This ritual helps with breaking the energy connection between two people but, if you need to follow-up in the mundane world for your safety, do so!

You Will Need

Two Chime, Spell, or Taper Candles - Any color will work, but black is especially good for banishing and protection.

A Length of Cord - Thread will work, just make sure it is a natural material that won't emit toxins when it burns. Cotton butcher string and hemp twine work very well.

Heat Proof Dish - A cast iron cauldron, skillet, or baking pan work well. This container may get hot so be sure the surface under your dish will not be damaged by the heat.

Sand - This is optional, see instructions

Matches or a Lighter

The Magic Begins

One of the candles represents you, the other represents the person with whom you are breaking ties. Put your own energy into your candle by holding it and focusing your intent. You can roll the candle up and down your body to imbue it with your energy. You might want to carve your initials into it or anoint it with your perfume. You can attach a piece of your hair to your candle, or put some under it when you place it in the container.

Connect the second candle to the other person by carving their initials into it, anointing it with their favorite scent, or attaching a piece of their hair to it. If you don't have any of their hair or fragrance, hold the candle up to your face and say something the other person frequently said that still burns in your thoughts. Focus your intent and recall all of the reasons you are putting this person out of your life and out of your mind.

Sit in a relaxed position with all the materials in front of you. You can light incense if you wish to set the mood, and allow yourself to relax. Tie the candles together with the string as indicated in the picture. Place the candles next to each other in the pan or cauldron. You can do this by warming the bottom of the candles with a lighter, and while the wax is soft press it into the pan, or use chime candle holders. Alternately, you can fill a dish or cauldron with some sand and stick the candles into the sand so they stay upright.

As you light each candle, speak your intent aloud. If you prefer, you can say these words of power:

> *The bonds are broken, I am free.*
> *You have no power over me.*
> *With all the power of three times three,*
> *This is my will, so mote it be.*

Allow the candles to burn down all the way. Again, make sure this is in a safe area away from curtains or flammable materials, and stick around to supervise. You don't have to stay sitting in front of them, but leave them out where you'll be able to monitor the progress of their burning. I often leave these long-burning spells on my altar, in the bathtub, or in the kitchen sink. As you periodically see the candles burning, reinforce your intent and repeat the words of power as above. At some point the string will catch on fire. If it doesn't by the time the candles are half-way burned, go ahead and light the string on fire while repeating the words of power and really focusing your willpower and intent. As the cord burns, your energy connection to this person is severed.

If one candle goes out, ask yourself if you are holding onto any desire for this person to stay in your life and make sure you have let go completely. Relight the candle while reinforcing your will and intent to banish this person from your life. When both candles have burned down and gone out, let any remaining wax or bits of string cool and solidify. Collect the remains and bury them, burn them in a campfire, or throw them away. It is done! Don't give this person any further energy by keeping them in your thoughts.

Magical Oils for Rituals, Anointing, & Perfume

E = Essential Oil, A = Absolute, gtt/gtts = Drop/Drops

Dilute all recipes with equal parts of a base oil such as jojoba, almond, avocado, apricot, or olive. An example is the first recipe with a total of 26 drops of essential oils and absolutes. Dilute this with an additional 26 drops of jojoba oil. The stone in parenthesis is a suggested addition to the bottle for extra energy.

Oil to Attract Friendship (Rose Quartz)
3 gtts Rose A | 20 gtts Sandalwood E
2 gtts Cinnamon E, 1 gtt Lavender E

Oil for Lustful Attraction (Garnet)
Create the Oil of Friendship Attraction above and add:
1 gtt Patchouli E | 1 gtt Jasmine A | 1 gtt Violet A

Oil for Purification & Banishing (Selenite or Kyanite)
This oil can be used in oil diffusers, as a personal fragrance, or used to anoint doorways and window ledges to cleanse the home.
12 gtts Atlas Cedar E | 10 gtts Clary Sage E | 10 gtts Frankincense E
15 gtts Rosemary E | 20 gtts Sandalwood E

Oil for Money, Prosperity, and Business (Aventurine)
1 gtt Violet A | 1 gtt Rose A | 3 gtts Cinnamon E
3 gtts Spearmint | 10 gtts Cedar | 3 gtts Carnation (optional)

Uncrossing Oil for Removing Hexes (Kyanite or Tourmaline)
3 gtts Clary Sage E | 3 gtts Rosemary E | 1 gtt Opopanax E
20 gtts Atlas Cedar E | 1 gtt Thyme E | 10 gtts Frankincense E

Good Luck Oil (Aventurine)
1 gtt Violet A | 1 gtt Rose A | 1 gtt Patchouli E
1 gtt Narcissus A | 10 gtts Spearmint E

Psychic Third-Eye Oil (Lapis Lazuli, Amethyst, or Sodalite)
5 gtts Rosemary E| 10 gtts Frankincense E | 1 gtt Rose A
3 gtts Opopanax E | 1 gtt Star Anise E | 20 gtts Sandalwood E
Add a very small nugget of Dragon's Blood resin to the bottle. Use a piece that would fit in a ⅛-¼ teaspoon measuring spoon.

The Directories

This section of your almanac contains the magical, metaphysical, and spiritual associations of plants and stones along with quick references to the meanings of runes and tarot cards. These directories maintain the perennial value of your almanac long after 2022.

Theban Script

A	B	C	D	E	F	G
H	I	J	K	L	M	N
O	P	Q	R	S	T	U
V	W	X	Y	Z		

Botanical Correspondences

Information on herbs, roots, resins, and other botanicals has been expanded to include notes from my personal book of shadows based on decades of experience. Rather than repeat information easily found online and in the many volumes of correspondence books, I've included some tips and accurate binomial (scientific) names of a few plants that are most frequently misidentified in herbals and Witchcraft books.

Acorn *Quercus spp*[25] - Protection, Strength, Luck. Acorns are perfect natural amulets. Carry an acorn for protection, or place around doors and windows to protect your home.

Adam & Eve Root *Aplectrum hyemale* - Happiness, Unification, Love. Although called "root" this is the tuber of an orchid. Two roots in a red pouch anointed with attraction oil will draw in relationship opportunities.

Adders Tongue *Erythronium americanum* - Calming, Healing, Soothing, Nurturing, Balancing (a.k.a. Trout Lily)

Agrimony - Virility, Banishing, Healing, Protection, Sleep

Ague Root (Unicorn Root) *Aletris farinosa* - Dreams, Ancestral Work, Hex-Breaking, Veil Lifting, Protection, Astral Travel (try a little in incense blends)

Alfalfa - Anti-hunger, Money, Victory, Prosperity

Alkanet *Alkanna tinctoria* - Prosperity, Purification. Powdered alkanet root can be mixed with oil and used as a red stain for runes, altar tools, tarot boxes, etc. I recommend using linseed (boiled flax seed) or teak oil as a base. Mix the powder with the oil and allow to steep for several days. Be sure to read all instructions on your oil container. An ink can be made by mixing the powder with alcohol and allowing to steep for several weeks (a Lunar cycle is best). Filter and use a glass dip pen to avoid clogging your fountain pen nibs.

Allspice - Healing, Luck, Money

Almond - Prosperity, Banishing Addictions, Money, Wisdom, Clarity

Aloe *Aloe spp.* - Healing, Soothing, Calming, Purification, Luck, Protection

Aloeswood (Agarwood or Oud) - *Aquilaria spp.* tree heartwood infected with the mold *Phialophora parasitica* - Used in incense for any spiritual or magical purpose. High spiritual vibrations are uplifting while also being grounding and empowering. Used primarily in incense and perfume, its sweet, balsamic, amber, woodsy, fragrance is difficult to describe.

---

25 Spp. and sp. are binomial abbreviations for multiple species (spp.) and singular species (sp.).

Alyssum - Blessing, Charm, Sweetening Your Perceptions, Balance, Protection. Excellent support for bees and pollinators.

Amaranth - Prosperity, Protection, Abundance, Healing, Veiling

Angelica Root - Hex-Breaking, Exorcism, Spell Reversal, Un-Crossing, Purification, Protection, Banishing, Visions

Anise - Banishing, Blessing, Divination, Hex-Reversal, Protection (similar to evil eye protection), Anti-Nightmare, Sleep, Peace, Meditation

Apple - Blessing, Friendship, Memory, Healing, Immortality, Love

Apricot - Love, Lust, Divination

Ash *Fraxinus spp.* - Spirituality, Wisdom, Choices, Strength, Divination, Health, Prosperity, Protection. Associated with Yggdrasil and easy to carve it makes a great wood for runes (as does Oak).

Aspen - Communication, Fortitude, Anti-Theft, Cleverness, Eloquence

Avocado - Fertility, Abundance, Beauty, Love, Lust

Bamboo - Strength, Resiliency, Abundance, Hex-Breaking, Luck, Protection,

Banana - Fertility, Potency, Virility Prosperity

Basil - Purification, Exorcism, Fidelity, Honesty, Love, Protection, Wealth

Bay - Healing, Protection, Psychic Powers, Blessing, Purification, Strength, Wishes, Manifestation

Bayberry - Success, Prosperity, Abundance, Money, Protection, Business

Benzoin - Prosperity, Abundance, Money, Clarity, Success, Purification, Blessing, Love

Bergamot - Prosperity, Abundance, Blessing

Birch - Exorcism, Protection, Purification

Black Cohosh - Courage, Love, Potency, Protection

Black Pepper - Spell-Reversal, Clarity, Banishing, Protection, Seeing the Truth, Energy

Blackberry - Faeries, Healing, Prosperity, Protection

Boneset - Healing, Banishing, Exorcism, Protection

Borage - Courage, Happiness, Psychic Powers

Buckthorn - Exorcism, Victory, Legal Success, Protection, Wishes

Cabbage - Abundance, Prosperity, Luck, Health

Camphor - Purification, Cleansing, Divination, Healing

Cannabis - Healing, Dreams, Meditation, Visions, Divination, Astral Projection, Creativity, Happiness, Stress Reduction, Love, Friendship, Calming, Soothing, Releasing

Caraway - Anti-Theft, Health, Lust, Mental Powers, Protection

Cardamon - Attraction, Stimulating, Love, Lust

Carnation - Money and Prosperity, Healing, Protection, Strength

Cascara Sagrada (Bearberry) *Frangula purshiana* - Legal Success, Victory, Money, Protection

Catnip - Friendship, Love, Lust, Beauty, Cat Magic, Happiness

Cedar - Purification, Banishing, Blessing, Exorcism, Abundance, Grounding, Healing, Money

Chamomile - Blessing, Peace, Dreams, Divination, Astral Projection, Love, Money, Purification, Sleep

Cherry - Divination, Love

Chickweed - Blessing, Fertility, Love

Chicory - Acceptance, Veiling, Removing Obstacles

Chili Peppers and Cayenne - Banishing, Fidelity, Hex-Breaking, Lust, Passion, Love, Strength, Purification, Exorcism, Seeing Truth, Clarity

Cinnamon - Abundance, Money and Prosperity, Healing, Love, Lust, Power, Protection, Psychic Powers, Spirituality, Success

Cinquefoil - Money and Prosperity, Prophetic Dreams, Protection, Sleep

Clove - Exorcism, Love, Money, Protection, Stops Gossip, Promotes Harmony, Healing. Clove works especially well to stop gossip when combined with mint or pennyroyal.

Clover (red or white) - Money and Prosperity, Success, Luck, Business, Exorcism, Fidelity, Love, Protection

Comfrey - Healing, Safe Travel, Money and Prosperity

Copal - Purification, Banishing, Cleansing, Protection, Blessing, Love

Coriander - Healing, Love, Enchantment

Cumin - Exorcism, Healing, Protection

Curry - Healing, Purification, Protection, Inner Strength

Cyclamen - Fertility, Happiness, Lust, Protection, sacred to Hecate

Cypress - Comfort, Grief Support, Healing, Longevity, Protection, Endurance

Damiana - Enchantment, Love, Lust, Visions

Dandelion - Healing, Protection, Strength, Calling Spirits, Divination, Wishes

Datura - Spell Reversal, Hex Breaking, Protection, Sleep

Dill - Luck, Lust, Money and Prosperity, Protection, Success, Eloquence

Dock - Fertility, Healing, Money

Dodder - Binding, Spell and Hex Stopping, Divination, Knot Magic, Love, Draining Power from Enchanted Items

Dragon's Blood - Power, Energy, Protection, Exorcism, Love, Potency, Courage, Strength, lust. Adds power to any energy work (Magical Catalyst).

Echinacea - Healing, Defense, Protection, Strength, Power

Elder - Exorcism, Wisdom, Healing, Divination, Prosperity, Protection, Sleep

Eucalyptus - Purification, Cleansing, Clarity, Healing, Protection

Fennel - Courage, Healing, Protection, Purification

Feverfew - Protection, Healing, Psychic Attack Prevention
Fig - Abundance, Divination, Fertility, Love
Flax - Divination, Beauty, Healing, Money, Blessing, Protection, Psychic Powers
Frankincense - Purification, Exorcism, Blessing, Protection, Spirituality
Galangal - Power, Energy, Healing, Hex and Spell Reversal, Lust, Money, Protection, Success, Vitality, Psychic Powers (similar to Ginger root)
Gardenia - Healing, Love, Peace, Spirituality
Garlic - Banishing, Protection, Purification, Anti-Theft, Seeing the Truth, Exorcism, Healing
Ginger - Power, Healing, Reversals, Love, Money, Power, Protection, Success (similar to Galangal)
Ginseng - Power, Energy, Strength, Courage, Healing, Love, Lust, Longevity, Protection, Wishes, Beauty
Gum Arabic - Protection, Friendship, Psychic Powers, Meditation, Consecration
Hawthorn - Protection, Magical Barriers, Happiness, Blessing, Warding
Henna - Magical Protection, Blessing, Enchantment, Beauty, Healing
Hibiscus - Energy, Divination, Dreams, Love, Lust
Hickory - Success, Eloquence, Strength, Legal Matters
High John the Conquerer - Protection, Success, Prosperity, Happiness, Love, Money, Anti-Hex
Holly - Protection, Magical Barriers, Dream Magic, Dreams, Luck, Longevity, Renewal
Honeysuckle - Seduction, Love, Lust, Money, Protection, Dreams
Hops - Balance, Dreams, Grounding, Healing, Sleep
Horse Chestnut - Luck, Health, Money and Prosperity, Memory, Love, Success. A horse chestnut seed is carried as a natural amulet for these intentions.
Hyssop - Cleansing, Purification, Protection
Irish Moss - Money and Prosperity, Luck, Protection
Ivy - Binding, Healing, Protection
Jasmine - Abundance, Love, Attracts Beneficial Relationships, Friendship, Money, Prophetic Dreams
Juniper - Purification, Cleansing, Exorcism, Health, Love, Protection
Lavender - Dreams, Calming, Happiness, Longevity, Love, Peace, Protection, Purification, Sleep
Lemon - Friendship, Longevity, Love, Purification
Lemon Balm - Clarity, Love, Lust, Friendship, Purification, Protection, Healing, Abundance, Success, Business
Lemon Verbena - Blessing, Purification, Attraction and Drawing, Love, Lust

Lemongrass - Clarity, Purification, Blessing, Protection, Divination
Licorice - Grounding, Protection, Healing, Fidelity, Love, Lust
Lilac - Exorcism, Faeries, Protection, Happiness, Memory
Lily of the Valley - Happiness, Balance, Memory
Lime - Healing, Love, Protection
Linden - Immortality, Love, Luck, Protection, Sleep
Liquidamber - Purification, Blessing, Protection, Personal Power, Magic Catalyst
Lotus - Divination, Dreams, Ancestral Work, Astral Projection, Meditation, Removing Obstacles
Lucky Hand - Business, Victory, Employment, Luck, Success, Money, Protection, Travel
Mace - Mental Powers, Clarity, Psychic Powers, Dreams, Psychic Powers
Mandrake (American) *Podophyllum peltatum* a.k.a. Mayapple - Protection, Money, Divination, Victory, Banishing, Veiling (hiding)
Mandrake & Womandrake (European) *Mandragora Spp.* - Magical Catalyst and Power Boost, Divination, Dreams, Crossing the Veil, Fertility, Banishing, Health, Victory, Love, Money, Protection. *M. officinarum* (Mandrake) and *M. autumnalis* (Womandrake or Autumn Drake) share similar correspondences and are often paired for love magic in place of poppets[26].
Maple - Divination, Psychic Powers, Peace, Longevity, Harmony, Love, Money
Marigold *Calendula officinalis* - Healing, Legal Matters, Victory, Prophetic Dreams, Courage, Purification, Protection, Happiness, Psychic Powers
Marigold (African & French) *Tagetes spp.* - Rub the dried leaves or flowers to release the pungent fragrance for Protection, Grounding, Purification, Clarity
Marjoram - Happiness, Health, Love, Money, Protection
Marshmallow (Althea Root or Mallow) *Althaea officinalis* - Carried to promote Prosperity and Opportunities, Burned for working with Spirits. Protection, Calming, Happiness, Positive Vibes, Psychic Powers
Masterwort (Ground Elder) *Aegopodium podagraria* - Many genus and species are referred to as "masterwort" but this is the one used in magic for Healing, Purification, Exorcism, Anti-Hex, Un-Crossing, Courage, Clarity
Mastic (Tears of Chios) *Pistacia lentiscus* - Resin from the mastic tree is used for incense in Purification, Healing, Positive Vibes, Lust, Manifestations, Psychic Powers. Fresh resin smells bad when burned but is soft and can be chewed like gum. When exposed to air

---

26 A poppet is a figure or doll used to focus magical energy.

and oxidized for several months it has a unique copal/benzoin type fragrance when burned.

Mesquite - Purification, Blessing, Healing

Mimosa - Love, Visions, Prophetic Dreams, Creativity, Purification

Mint (peppermint, spearmint, etc.) - Abundance, Money and Prosperity, Purification, Exorcism, Healing, Love, Lust, Safe Travel, Clarity, Memory

Mistletoe - Blessing, Enchanting, Exorcism, Fertility, Health, Hunting, Love, Protection

Morning Glory - Binding, Acceptance, New Beginnings, Happiness

Mugwort - Astral Projection, Ancestral Work, Divination, Dreams, Healing, Prophetic Dreams, Protection, Psychic Powers, Strength

Mulberry - Courage, Protection, Strength

Mullein - Dreams, Visions, Courage, Divination, Exorcism, Health, Love, Protection

Mustard - Fertility, Mental Powers, Protection, Disenchantment

Myrrh - Banishing, Purification, Exorcism, Healing, Protection, Spirituality, Blessing, Prosperity

Nettle - Healing, Banishing, Exorcism, Protection

Norfolk Island Pine - Protection, Weight Loss, Craving Reduction (Keep one potted in your kitchen or near your ash tray.)

Nutmeg - Clarity, Focus, Seeing the Truth

Oak - Victory, Strength, Endurance, Control, Fertility, Healing, Luck, Money, Potency, Protection

Olive - Peace, Fertility, Healing, Lust, Protection

Onion - Exorcism, Healing, Lust, Money, Prophetic Dreams, Protection

Orange - Divination, Love, Luck, Money

Oregon Grape - Abundance, Money and Prosperity, Healing

Orris Root - Harmony, Complex Energy Work (where blending drawing and repelling is necessary), Divination, Love, Protection

Parsley - Money, Love, Protection, Purification

Passion Flower - Balance, Dreams, Visions, Passion, Lust, Love, Divination, Friendship, Peace, Sleep

Patchouli - Protection, Blessing, Money, Lust, Attraction

Peach - Exorcism, Longevity, Divination, Fertility, Love, Wishes

Pear - Fertility, Love, Lust

Pennyroyal - Breaking Addictions, Astral Work, Business, Ending Gossip, Peace, Protection, Strength. Pennyroyal works especially well to stop gossip when combined with clove.

Periwinkle *Vinca minor* - Clarity, Memory, Love, Lust, Mental Powers, Money, Protection

Pine - Cleansing, Purification, Blessing, Exorcism, Fertility, Healing, Money, Protection

Plantain - Healing, Strength, Protection

Plumeria (Frangipani) - Love, Happiness, Energy, Friendship

Pomegranate - Divination, Fertility, Luck, Wealth, Wishes, Persephone, Wisdom
Poppy - Veiling, Creativity, Love, Luck, Money, Sleep
Raspberry - Healing, Love, Protection, Cooperation
Rose - Blessing, Divination, Dreams, Happiness, Healing, Love, Luck, Protection, Psychic Powers, Enchantment
Rosemary - Purification, Cleansing, Blessing, Clarity, Exorcism, Love, Lust, Memory, Mental Acuity, Divination
Rowan (European Mountain Ash) *Sorbus aucuparia and Sorbus spp.* - Healing, Power, Protection, Psychic Powers, Success
Rue *Ruta graveolens* - Protection, Power, Exorcism, Healing, Strength, Love, Clarity, Fortitude, Courage. Wear a sprig to prevent being influenced by others, or to honor Diana, Aradia, Selene, Hecate, and other moon Goddesses. Contact with the fresh herb can cause photo-sensitivity (stay out of the sun). Cimaruta (chee-mah-roo-tah) are silver rue sprig charms worn by Stregheria and other Witches.

Saffron (Autumn Crocus) *Crocus sativus* - Power, Energy, Happiness, Purification, Spirituality, Balance, Healing, Love, Lust, Psychic Powers, Strength, Protection, Wind Raising. Saffron and Aloeswood are probability the two most costly botanicals on this list (rivaling medical marijuana). The availability of saffron will be decreasing over the next few years and its price will skyrocket. Luckily, it is easy to grow, providing carefree flowers. When you purchase *Crocus sativus* bulbs, be sure to verify the binomial, as other species sold as "Autumn Crocus" are toxic. Short purple flowers are hardy perennials to 14°F (-10° Celsius), and their leaves look similar to grass. Each flower has three saffron strands, but that is all you need to flavor an entire rice dish when the strands are fresh.
Sage (Garden Sage) *Salvia officinalis* - Purification, Cleansing, Immortality, Wisdom, Longevity, Protection, Clarity
Sandalwood - Blessing, Peace, Purification, Meditation, Spirit and Ancestral Work, Healing, Astral Travel, Un-Crossing, Protection, Banishing
Sarsaparilla - Love, Lust, Prosperity
Sassafras - Protection, Prosperity, Divination, Dreams
Scullcap - Dreams, Calming, Visions, Astral Work, Divination, Love, Peace
Solomon's Seal - Warding, Banishing, Exorcism, Protection
Spanish Moss - Banishing, Success, Business, Protection
St John's Wort - Happiness, Balance, Strength, Optimism, Courage, Insight, Healing,

Star Anise - Blessing, Divination, Luck, Psychic Powers, Protection

Strawberry - Love, Lust, Abundance, Luck

Summer Savory - Clarity, Insight, Divination, Wisdom, Mental Powers. Combines synergistically with Rosemary and the combination is excellent for food magic in pasta and bean dishes.

Sunflower - Prosperity, Protection, Abundance, Fertility, Health, Wisdom

Sweat Pea - Cooperation, Friendship, Companionship

Sweetgrass - Ancestral Work, Welcoming and Calling Spirits, Blessing

Tansy - Health, Longevity, Protection. Brushing up against the plant can cause photo-sensitivity. Wash skin well after cultivating and harvesting, and stay out of the sun.

Tea (Green or Black) *Camellia sinensis* - Strength, Balance, Healing, Courage, Divination, Managing Fear, Soothing Grief, Prosperity

Thistle - Courage, Defense, Energy, Finances, Healing, hex Breaking, Protection, Strength

Thorn Root (Cat Brier, Dragon Root) *Smilax spp.* - Powerful Protection, Spell-Reversal, Anti-Hex, Banishing, Un-Crossing, Evil Eye type Protection. Thorn root can be used in any spell pouch or jar. Advanced wortcunning practitioners use Thorn Root to create Dragon Root[27], a unique magical ward. This is done in a special ritual that involves steeping the roots during specific lunar cycles in a tincture made of numerous herbs and resins (including Dragon's Blood resin). These unique wards seek out and absorb baneful magical and energy attacks, become stronger over time, and do not need to be cleansed or charged. They are hung in the home much like a Witch Ball or Kitchen Witch.

Thyme - Courage, Healing, Health, Love, Psychic Powers, Purification, Sleep

Turmeric - Healing, Protection, Strength, Clarity, Purification

Valerian - Consecration, Dreams, Love, Protection, Purification, Sleep, Anxiety Reduction

Vanilla - Prosperity, Friendship, Love, Lust, Clarity

Vervain - Chastity, Healing, Love, Money, Peace, Protection, Purification, Sleep, Youth, sacred to the Triple Goddess

Vetivert - Protection, Un-Crossing, Anti-Theft, Hex-Breaking, Luck, Prosperity, Attraction. Use vetivert oil in ritual oils and perfume designed for drawing. Add your intention to draw in money, love, opportunities, etc.

Violet - Money and Prosperity, Healing, Attraction, Love, Luck, Lust, Peace, Protection, Wishes

Willow - Happiness, Grief Support, Divination, Psychic Skills, Enchantment, Healing, Love, Protection, Blessing

---

27 The original instructions for this ritual are only at WitchAcademy.org

Wintergreen - Un-Crossing, Healing, Hex-Breaking, Protection
Witch Grass (couch grass) *Elymus repens* - Roots used in medieval northern Europe for incense in place of costly and scarce resins. Exorcism, Happiness, Love, Protection, Lust, Purification, Blessings
Witch Hazel - Healing, Protection, Wisdom
Wormwood - Calling Spirits, Ancestral Work, Divination, Love, Protection, Psychic Powers, Astral Projection. Wormwood is helpful when both invoking or dismissing energies and helps maintain clarity while in meditation, trance, or between the worlds.
Yarrow - Courage, Depression, Spell-Reversal, Divination, Truth Revealing, Clarity, Exorcism, Love, Psychic Powers, Influencing Others. Dried stems can be used for traditional I Ching.
Yew - Calling Spirits, Ancestral Work, Astral Projection, Dreams
Yerba Mate *Ilex paraguariensis* - Lust, Love, Divination, Energy, Virility, Clarity, Happiness
Yucca - Protection, Purification, Transmutation

Stones Crystals & Minerals

Stones are excellent tools for spells and magic. You can use them in pouches, carry them as an amulet, incorporate them into tools, and use them as wards. This correspondence list will help you select the stone that fits your needs. These stone profiles reflect our experiences, so please remember that you may feel a different energy from a type of stone and that every stone has its own 'personality'. Stones should not be disposed of after magical use. Cleanse and re-use! They've been around for hundreds of thousands, or even millions of years and their energy bounces back readily.

Amazonite: A type of feldspar used for harmony, blending many energies, peace, calm, communication.

Amber: Amber is one of the earliest 'stones' used by humans in religion and magic, and is a classic amulet used by Witches. It is considered a gemstone, but is not a mineral. Amber is the fossilized resin of ancient trees, and its use has been dated back to the Neolithic period. Solar and light energy. Very energizing, increases power, purification, and protection from negativity, psychic and magical vampirism; shielding (without hiding), healing, soothing, warming. Amber is often combined with jet.

Amethyst: Enhances general magical workings and raises personal power. To fine-tune its energy, combine amethyst with other stones and focus clearly on your goals and intent. Well suited to psychic development, protection, detoxification, inner exploration, emotional and psychic shielding, purification, breaking addictions, self-understanding.

Apache Tears: A special variety of volcanic obsidian used for protection and shielding, emotional cleansing, grounding. Brings protective earth energy to sensitive psychics and empaths.

Black Tourmaline: Protection and purification. Probably the best all-around protection stone. Tends to need less cleansing than many stones. Shielding, grounding, neutralizing, detoxification, prevents psychic and magical drain, anti-hex, converts negative energy into neutral energy.

Bloodstone: A red and green chalcedony used for strength, healing, courage, detoxification, purification. Very balancing, energizing and grounding of sexual and emotional centers for healing the body and spirit. Combines well with other stones and spell ingredients. (Works and plays well with others.)

Botswana Agate: Soothing and energizing, like a spa treatment for the spirit. For manifesting higher goals, clearing conflict, harmonizing, absorbs negative energy (cleanse stone well) and prevents unwanted visitors (physical, psychic, dimensional, etc.). Cuts ties to the past, psychic links, hexes, addictions & negative patterns. Helps prevent dwelling/obsessing on the negative; helps find solutions.

Carnelian: Orange-red and usually semi-translucent. For focus, concentration, uplifting, energizing, protection. Prevents psychic and emotional drain. Helps reinforce aura, increase confidence, improve motivation. Brings an energizing life force for creativity, personal will, and sexuality.

Celestite: Also known as Celestine, this rare mineral is used to help you connect with your higher self, tune-in to your deeper goals, face your fears, and for dream work. Very healing when working through issues in order to reclaim your personal power, and open your flow of energy to that of the universe. With time, this use also helps with manifestation of your true goals and desires in the physical plane.

Citrine: A quartz in the yellow hues, from lemon-yellow to root beer amber. Very energizing and enlightening. Used for manifestation of creativity. Brightens mood, boosts your 'inner fire' and protects against negativity.

Clear Quartz: Power, protection, harmony, energy. These powerhouses will boost the energy of any healing, energy work, ritual tool or talisman. Whether tumbled smooth or in their original pointed crystal form, they add their energy to the overall working according to your will and focus, while providing clarity and helping harmonize mixed energies of other stones, other people's wills, etc. Pictured is the crystalline growth of a cluster of crystals.

Fluorite: The color often indicates its uses, ranging from green (healing) to purple (psychic work) and more. Very high energy in the mind and crown chakra. It can help to open doors of perception, improve mental clarity for decision making, divination or study. Very cleansing and purifying, will remove negativity and is a great 'junk eraser' after healing, psychic, ritual, spell and magical work.

Garnet: Healing broken hearts, physical health, strength, sexual expression, self-worth, attraction, lust, sexual love, protection. Used to invoke the symbolism of the pomegranate. Earth energy, fertility.

Goldstone: Helps you focus on and achieve your goals; increases ambition and drive; emotionally stabilizing; protection; uplifting. Has a slight tendency to attract money.

Green Aventurine: A green quartz stone with mica inclusions. Increases opportunities, confidence, growth, personal energy, vitality, and perception. Aventurine is often used for luck; helping you take advantage of opportunities, and allowing you to better perceive opportunities as they arise. Traditionally used to attract adventure and for general attraction, creating a positive attitude, fortifying independence; said by some practitioners to invoke the favor of the Goddess of Love.

Hawk's Eye: A 'tiger's eye' stone in the colors of blue, green and gray. For clarity and gaining perspective, psychic work and visions, opening the third eye, protection while doing visualization, divination, and magic. Eye stones are often used for luck, helping you take advantage of opportunities, or helping you to perceive opportunities as they arise. Psychic, mental and emotional stamina.

Hematite: An iron oxide mineral. Manifestation, potency, charisma, grounding, balancing of opposites, detoxification, strength, and courage; can be used in spells for removing insecurity or even impotence.

Jasper: see Mook Jasper, Picture Jasper, Red Jasper

Jet: Like amber, jet is a very powerful amulet used since ancient times. One of the earliest stones used by humans, jet is a traditional Witch's amulet. Although jet is a gemstone, it is a mineraloid not a mineral. It comes from the wood from ancient coniferous trees that has been transformed over millions of years under extreme pressure. Used for protection, purification, manifesting your intentions on the physical plane, stress relief, grief support, dispelling negative patterns within and without, and grounding (without heaviness). Jet prevents psychic and magical vampirism and helps connect to earth and lunar energy. Jet is often combined with amber.

Kyanite: Mental and psychic clarity; stays clear for better purification and protection; quick access to visualization, magical powers, telepathy, and intuition. Unlocks the third eye, helps you understand how to use your skills responsibly. Aids in communication, expression, balance, dream work, meditation.

Lapis Lazuli: Creativity, visualization, expression, articulation, communication, intuition, useful for divination and psychic readings. Helps you tap into your psychic centers to aid in gathering and directing your energy, raising power for magic and spells, visualizing and manifesting goals.

Mahogany Obsidian: Promotes inner strength & healing; reduces feelings of unworthiness; amazing ability to end psychic attacks & psychic "chains" or "ties" placed either consciously or subconsciously by others. Stabilizing & grounding for better manifestation & healing. Unblocking, protection, gently grounding.

Malachite: Useful for analyzing repeated negative patterns, draws out repressed memories and emotions, good for revealing and healing emotional damage and trauma. Helps heal broken hearts.

Mook Jasper: A micro-crystalline quartz. Helps tune into earth energies, cycles, and patterns. Excellent for maintaining the sense of wonder and openness of youth, thereby increasing opportunities and a sense of gratitude.

Moonstone: Self-acceptance, self-confidence, tuning into your intuition and psychic centers, soothing, balancing and calming, dream work, facing fears, discovering truth, working with cycles and patterns, feminine power, intuition, Goddess energy, inspiration, creativity.

Picture Jasper: Banded with many colors, the patterns in the stone sometimes resemble a landscape. Tuning into earth energies, harmonizing multiple energies, gaining perspective and insight for physical manifestations (redecorating, garden plans, business plans). Visualization, nurturing, confidence.

Red Jasper: A micro-crystalline quartz. A very useful stone you will reach for again and again. Balancing, handling emotional stress, retaining dreams and visions, enhancing physical strength and inner stability. Gently grounding. Has good healing energy, especially in the lower chakra centers.

Red Tiger's Eye & Golden Cat's Eye: Found in red (tiger), gold and yellow (cat) and used for protection, perception, clear thinking, discovering the truth, and increasing luck. Like Aventurine, eye stones are often used for general luck, but this is primarily due to their ability to help you take advantage of opportunities by increasing your ability to perceive both opportunities and pitfalls as they arise. Excellent for enhancing and focusing your willpower, protection, grounding, vitality, motivation, balance, insight and integrity. Also used for psychic, mental and emotional stamina; and for seeing your way clearly.

Rhodonite: Pink and black coloration is a reminder of the grounding and centering of this stone's energy. It helps to stabilize emotions and ground the heart chakra for better healing. A stone of grace, discovering hidden talents, generosity, and compassion, expression of love, understanding your purpose.

Rose Quartz: Pink shades of micro-crystalline quartz, usually found in mass rather than individual crystals. Heals emotions, self-love & self-acceptance. Dissipates negativity, anger, tension & frustration. For unconditional love, self-acceptance, beauty, allowing love in, creativity; enhances receptivity to love; prevents fighting and encourages harmony, friendship, and peace. When combining multiple stones and crystals, rose quartz helps to harmonize their energies.

Ruby: Increases life force, courage, confidence; invokes sensuality and passion; attracts people towards the wearer. Energizes and acti-vates all energy centers; Boosts motivation; helps aspire to new levels.

Sapphire: Balancing, healing & soothing; Increases awareness and personal power. Said to ensure faithfulness and protect relationships from love triangles

Selenite: A soft stone with a powerful punch. Helps to direct energy to your will and goals, aids in communicating with other realms, clears the cobwebs from the third eye and crown to enhance percep-tion. Increase awareness, psychic skills & insight. Harmoniously blends & amplifies other stones.

Shiva Lingham: Meditation, insight, healing, very balancing & energizing, psychic skills, high spiritual vibrations, union of opposites, manifestation of wisdom. Healing of emotional and sexual issues, reclaiming sexual power and increasing self-love. Understanding and trusting the positive masculine.

Smokey Quartz: Protective of sensitive people, helping to guard against over-empathizing, being suckered by con artists, and helps prevent unhealthy relationships with others. Both grounding and uplifting, it is often used to move energy through all the seven major chakras. Pairs well with amethyst.

Snowflake Obsidian: You will love this stone so much that even after decades of use, you will find yourself coming back to it. While grounding, centering and protecting, it brings hidden things to the surface. You can use this energy for emotional and physical healing, psychic awareness and even for spells to return lost objects. Helps one to see patterns for better psychic readings and mental health.

Sodalite: A fantastic writer's stone for inspiration and any creative pursuit involving intelligence, communication, education (teaching and learning), creativity, foresight, and logic.

Spirit Quartz: Found in amethyst, clear and other types of quartz, these special formations are a larger crystal covered in many smaller druzy quartz crystals. Gaining perspective, increasing humor and ability to experience joy, reducing fears and anxiety, moving on, speeds and enhances magical workings, great for covens as it helps many people work toward a common goal, heals discord, increases patience, will receive a magical charge well, making it well suited to talismans and wards. Projects a charge well.

Staurolite Crystal: Also called a *fairy cross*. Symbolizes the crossing of paths on the universal web, invokes the favor of the Fates or Goddess of Crossroads. Helps protect against hexes, negativity & rebound from magical work and spells.

Tiger Iron: A very powerful combination of red jasper, tiger eye, and hematite. Harmoniously blends all of the energies of these three stones. Great for manifestation, protection, energy, strength, stamina, increases willpower, motivation, bringing insights into action, healing, and grounding, creative solutions.

Tourmalated Quartz: A powerful shield of protection and neutralization of negative energy. Stays clear a long time, making it perfect as a 'take with you' charm. Energizing and grounding at the same time. Good for purification.

Tourmaline: see Black Tourmaline

Unakite: A green and pink jasper (micro-crystalline quartz) that balances and heals the heart, helps manifest love, calms, stabilizing, prevents ego-based negative patterns, releasing.

Watermelon Tourmaline: Balances the heart, encourages self-love while healing and recovering from negative relationships or past mistakes. Increases your magnetism and attraction for your positive benefit. Tends to protect you from spells cast by others, but this energy is more prominent in black tourmaline.

Wavellite: A powerful mineral found in Arkansas near the place where some of the best magical quartz crystals come from. Extremely useful for tuning into earth energies, manifestation, understanding interconnections, healing emotions, finding your path and making decisions. Excellent for healing, increasing your sense of well-being, changing your perspective when you are feeling down or 'stuck' and helps you gain insight.

Zebra Stone: Helps you see yourself and others clearly. Grounds high energy without being too heavy, it helps to manifest goals on the material plane. Unconditional love, helps harmonize varied energies of numerous stones or ingredients in a spell or talisman. Combats depression, apathy, and disinterest; increases creativity and motivation; nurturing & protective energy.

Reading the Tarot's Roman Numerals

Have you ever wondered about those letters you see on major arcana tarot cards? They are Roman Numerals and even if you don't like math, you can read them by using this reference guide. I is one, V is five, and X is ten. When a letter appears twice it is doubled. For example, II is two and XX is twenty. The same goes for tripling, III is three and XXX is thirty.

If a letter with a lower value is to the **left** of a letter with a greater value, you subtract the lower from the greater. For example, IV = 5 (V) minus 1 (I) = 4 or IX = 10 (X) minus 1 (I) = 9.

When a letter of lower value is on the **right** of a letter with greater value, you add the lower to the greater. For example, VI = 5 (V) + 1 (I) = 6 and XI = 10 (X) + 1 (I) = 11.

Elder Futhark Runes

The Elder Futhark is used for divination, magic, and personal reflection. They can be used to inscribe tools or to develop sigils and bind-runes for magic. It is best to develop a good understanding of the runes before such uses, and utilizing them as a divination tool will help you gain the necessary insight. Next to each rune below is its name and English letter equivalent (transliteration), followed by an approximate pronunciation and a summary of each rune's meaning. Further study is recommended before divination use.

A blank rune is found in some sets but is not a historical part of the Elder Futhark. The Elder Futhark is 24 runes divided into three groups of eight (ættir). Recently, Ralph Blum popularized the use of a blank rune to represent "fate" or "destiny". To stick with tradition, just use blanks as spares in case you loose one of the traditional 24.

ᚠ	F	Fehu /fay-who/ Controlled power over wealth. Manifesting creative energy and power. Invest wisely to increase wealth
ᚢ	U	Uruz /oo-rooz/ Vital strength, primal power, determination health, perseverance, manifestation, wisdom & lore
ᚦ	TH þ	Thurisaz /thoor-ee-sahs/ Thorn, protection, fence, barrier, enemy of baneful forces, defense, destruction, applied power
ᚨ	A	Ansuz /ahn-sooz/ Breath, word/song, incantations, shaping power or sound, expression, communication
ᚱ	R	Raidho /rye-thoh/ Riding, wheel, journey and travel, quest, change, ritual, rhythm, movement, order, the underworld
ᚲ	K	Kenaz /kane-ahz/ Torch, light, fires of transformation, passion, illumination, regeneration, enlightenment, kinship
ᚷ	G	Gebo /gay-boh/ Gift, exchange of powers, relationships, exchanges, crossing paths or uniting, connections, balance
ᚹ	W or V	Wunjo /woon-yo/ Joy, perfection, shared goals, harmony of like forces, best traits of all combined as a force, happiness

ᚺ	H	Hagalaz /haw-gah-lahs/ Hail, hailstone, disruption, destruction, seed form, moving ice, overcome hardship
ᚾ	N	Naudhiz /now-theez/ Need, necessity, distress, necessity is the mother of invention, resistance, friction→fire
ᛁ	I	Isa /ee-sah/ Ice, contraction, stillness, suspension, introspection, restraint, slowed growth, stagnation
ᛃ	J or Y	Jera /yur-ah/ Harvest, year, season, cycle, the flow of life-death-rebirth, fruition, completion, sow/reap
ᛇ	E	Eihwaz /ii-wahz/ ï (æ) Yew tree, world axis, endings/beginnings, opportunity, passage, between, protection
ᛈ	P	Perthro /pear-throh/ Dice cup, vulva, birth, problem-solving, evolutionary force, chance, destiny
ᛉ	Z	Elhaz /ale-hawz/ or /all-geese/ Elk, protection, defense, support, luck, shielding, sanctuary, deity connection
ᛋ	S	Sowilo /soh-wil-oh/ or /so-woo-loh/ Sun, will, strength, victory, success, vitality, healing, solar energy and movement, directing power, clarity
ᛏ	T	Tiwaz /tee-wahz/ Creator, justice, success, responsibility, will, guided to success-truth-victory-justice-a good path, law & order
ᛒ	B	Berkano /bear-kahn-oh/ Birch tree, birch twig, life-death-rebirth, regeneration, growth, intuition, female fertility, new beginnings
ᛖ	E	Ehwaz /ay-wahz/ or /ay-woh/ Horse, movement, connections, connecting with another force to achieve a goal
ᛗ	M	Mannaz /mahn-nahz/ Man (human), exam, dispute, challenge, arguments, gaining upper hand, communication.
ᛚ	L	Laguz /lah-gooz/ Water, lake, flowing, emotion, intuition, psychic power, revealing what is hidden
ᛜ	NG ŋ	Ingwaz /eeng-wahz/ Fertility, Frey, potential energy, opportunity, how endings affect beginnings
ᛟ	O	Othala /oath-ah-lah/ Home, sacred ancestral land, inherited land, inheritance, ancestral power, true wealth and treasures (rather than currency).

You can create your own runes with disks of wood, paper, or clay. As you form each rune confirm its meaning.

Tarot Meanings

These interpretations were developed over decades of practice and thousands of readings. You can use these to supplement your own keywords for each card.

The first part of each meaning is for the upright position, but the essence of this meaning is always present no matter what position the card is drawn. The second part, marked with **R:**, is for the reversed or upside-down meaning of a card. Remember that the upright meaning still influences the reading, even when the card is reversed.

An example of this is the Wheel of Fortune drawn in reversed position. Most readers would say that this means "bad luck." However, luck can change, and just the mere presence of the Wheel indicates that things could be turned around. Look to the other cards in a spread (layout of tarot cards) to determine how this turn can occur.

Major Arcana

0 The Fool The Fool has no numeric designation and "travels" through the tarot as indicated by the Arabic numeral zero instead of the usual Roman numerals. Playfulness, Childlike, Adventurous, spontaneous **R:** Foolish - Naive - Overly Optimistic, not looking before you leap, hiding from the truth

I Magician Self Confidence, Arcana, secrets & occult study, Showmanship, show off, talented performer, meeting of fate **R:** Manipulation, Insecurity, Trickery, Lies, A Player, smarmy

THE FOOL.

II High Priestess Experience, Wisdom, Intuition, psychic skills, Learning, Teacher **R:** Using knowledge without wisdom - Hysterical, unbalanced, out of control - Severe low self-esteem, not trusting what your intuition is telling you

III Empress Motherly, Growth, Nurturing, Abundance, being "mom" to everyone **R:** Shallow, Greedy - Ignoring the bigger picture - Motherly Problems

IV Emperor Order, rules, laws, authority figure, boss, getting organized **R:** Impractical, Narrow-minded, Control freak, need to get organized, toxic masculinity

V Hierophant Following Tradition - Conventional - Getting good Counsel **R:** Counseling needed - Think for yourself – Unorthodox, finding spirituality in alternative paths

VI Lovers Love & Romance, Sharing, Equal Partnership **R:** Separation, Arguments, Incompatible Partner, different goals

VII Chariot Travel, Movement, Drive, Ambition **R:** Procrastination, Delays, Obstacles, Can't move forward, car trouble

VIII Strength Confident, In Control, Gaining Inner Strength, Strength born out of trauma **R:** Drained, Depression, Co-dependent, Fear of standing on your own

IX Hermit Meditation, Re-evaluate, Alone by choice Finding answers in yourself **R:** Unwanted loneliness, Need to re-evaluate, Isolation, Withdrawn, Anxiety

X Wheel of Fortune Prosperity, Promotions, Luck, Windfalls, Paid your dues **R:** Stuck in a rut, Refusing change, Not taking chances, Down on luck (but the wheel will turn again)

XI Justice Legal matters (good), Fair treatment, Karma **R:** Legal matters (disappointing or delayed), Unfair treatment

XII Hanged Man Suspension, Waiting, Calm before the Storm, Between **R:** Delays, Indecision. Hang Ups, Impatient
XIII Death Major changes - New outlook - Letting go **R:** Fear of change - Living in the past - Need to let go

XIV Temperance Patience, Compromise, Tolerance, Control, understanding degrees of intensity **R:** Need moderation, patience or compromise

XV Devil Obsession, Infatuation, Lust Materialism, Addiction, Willingly chained to the material realm **R:** Facing Fears - Overcoming all of the above

XVI Tower Chaos, Sudden Change (a needed change) Destruction (out of which comes rebirth and truth) **R:** Chaos Ending, Time to grow and move on, Rebuild with a clean slate

XVII Star Hope, Focusing on dreams & goals, Finding your true path **R:** Losing hope, Disillusioned, Depressed

XVIII Moon Something hidden from them or they are hiding something. Insecurity, Visions **R:** Deception, Something hidden (truth?) - Insecurity – Misunderstandings

XIX Sun New Beginnings, Success, Happiness, Birth, Children, Family, Health **R:** Delayed beginnings, Feeling Unfulfilled, Family trouble, Weariness

XX Judgement Good Karma, Rewards, Making fair and logical decisions **R:** Bad Karma, Poor Judgment, Need to be e practical and fair

XXI World Endings & New Beginnings, Cycles, Success, Expanding Horizons **R:** Delay in a Cycle Ending, Accept Changes, Complete projects before starting new ones

Minor Arcana

Swords: Conflicts, The Mind, Thoughts

Ace of Swords

Ace Beginnings, New Ideas, projects, Medical (surgery, injection, cut) **R:** Delays in new beginnings (cut out the past) Overbearing, Confusion, Medical(surgery, injection, cut)
Two Stubborn, No compromises, Battle of wills, Can't see a way out, Standstill **R:** Reconciliation, Compromise, Two things reuniting (ideas, people, etc.)
Three Love triangle, Jealousy, Heartache, Medical (surgery, injection, cut) **R:** Recovering from above, Medical (surgery, injection, cut)
Four Taking some "ME" time, Recovery, Rest, Take time off, Recuperate **R:** Recovery almost complete, Need to take some "ME" time
Five Finding out who your true friends are, Gossip, Deceit, Hidden or old enemies **R:** Finding out who your true friends are Gossip ending, Truth revealed
Six Moving on, Letting go, travel, following your own path **R:** Frying pan into the fire - moving on in a bad direction
Seven Being Used, Theft, Trickery, lies, rip-off, doesn't trust (and maybe shouldn't) **R:** Not allowing yourself to be used, Evening the score, Stolen property returned
Eight Walking on eggshells, can't speak your mind **R:** Starting to speak your mind, Fear of independence

Nine Sleepless Nights, Worried, Stress, Illness? (reproductive system?) Worried Sick; Female Energy **R:** Light at the end of a tunnel, recovery, burden lifted, beginning to feel less stress
Ten Betrayal, Stab in the back, Landing flat on your face **R:** Learning from mistakes or betrayal, getting back on feet
Page Communicate, be direct to avoid serious misunderstandings, News (good) R: News (bad), Angry (with father?)
Knight Intelligent, changes coming quickly & unexpectedly **R:** violence, fights, sudden changes
Queen Sharp mind, sharp tongue, clever & helpful **R:** Bitter, mean spirited woman who knows just what to say to hurt you the most
King Sharp mind, sharp tongue, clever & helpful **R:** Nasty & mean spirited man, abusive

Cups, Goblets, or Chalices: Emotions, The Heart, Love & Relationships

Ace of Cups

Ace New relationships, birth **R:** New relationships delayed, next step delayed, pregnancy trouble
Two Equal and balanced relationship, feelings are mutual **R:** Unbalanced relationship, feelings are not reciprocated
Three Celebrations, parties, going out, no serious relationship, family gatherings **R:** Overindulgence, heavy partying, bad family gatherings, addiction
Four Not satisfied, not realizing the value of the current love, Bored **R:** Seeing the value of current love, becoming satisfied with a relationship, focusing too much on what has been lost rather than what exists
Five A loss but something left standing to rebuild on, focusing too much on the loss **R:** Same as above, but starting to focus on recovery
Six Family, memories, the past returning with new meaning **R:** Living in the past, outgrowing a relationship or person
Seven Too many dreams without plans to get them, choose a path or person, idealism **R:** Deciding what you want, making plans & setting realistic priorities, focusing on one path out of many options
Eight Leaving the past (loss & love) behind, some temporary loneliness **R:** Yo-yo relationships, settling for a relationship that isn't good
Nine Achieved goals and dreams, but now a bit bored **R:** Smug, Not quite accomplishing goals because they are unrealistic
Ten Wishes & Dreams coming true, love and family surrounding, comfort **R:** Happiness coming, but delayed, trouble getting a commitment

Page Loving person, student, Reflect & look inside yourself for inspiration & love **R:** Unloving person, need for reflection
Knight Love coming, Person who changes partners frequently **R:** Love going, past heartaches fading into the past
Queen Kind, gentle, soft-spoken, loving woman **R:** Hysterical, emotional, oversensitive, easily taken advantage of, unloving
King Fair, gentle, loving & caring man, great father figure **R:** Weak, unreliable man, cheater

Wands, Rods, or Staves: Communication, Ideas, Friendships, Expression of Thoughts, Movement

Ace New Creativity, Communication (letter, call, email) **R:** Feeling uncreative, uninspired, no communication (letter, call, email)
Two Best friendship, equal relationship, great communication, long-distance relationship **R:** Two people with different ideas and goals, incompatibility, miscommunication
Three Counseling, a third party helps (doctor, friend, shared work) **R:** Third party interfering (inlaws, boss, etc.) Someone in the way
Four Stability, marriage, firm foundation **R:** Non-marital commitment, living together, living with roommates
Five Battles & arguments have good results, solutions found through fights **R:** Battles & arguments do not result in solutions
Six Victory, winning battles, overcoming stress **R:** Defeat, disillusioned, rewards and victory delayed
Seven Attacked from all sides, learning to communicate well & win battles **R:** Attacked from all sides and feeling drained & stressed
Eight Expanding horizons through travel, talking to people or seeing new places, reading new ideas **R:** Frustration and delays, can't seem to communicate
Nine Battles are behind you now, ready & prepared for what is ahead, good at communicating **R:** Paranoid from many past battles, defensive (Jail? Prison?)
Ten Responsibilities you love to have, promotions, kids, rewards for hard work ahead **R:** Overburdened, too many responsibilities, rewards ahead - remain strong
Page Travel, news, communications, email, letters, phone calls **R:** Delays or problems in the above
Knight Person with an inner fire, great ideas, good at communicating **R:** Jumping from idea to idea, need for follow through
Queen Talkative & creative woman, full of fire and passion **R:** Gossipy, burns out quickly

King Talkative & creative man, very reliable and great to talk to **R:** Unreliable, forked tongue

Pentacles, Coins, or Disks: Money, Material Things, Practical Matters

Ace New Job, Money coming, Ideas for making money, Begin new projects! **R:** Timing isn't right yet for new projects, Delays with money

Two Juggling money or jobs, business partnership **R:** Trouble juggling money or jobs, distracted

Three Making money from an area of expertise, craftsmanship, journeyman **R:** Not using your skills so not making potential $

Four Financial stability, but too afraid to take risks or enjoy $ (insecurity) **R:** Greedy, stingy, extremely insecure and using money and material stuff as a security blanket

Five Feeling left out in the cold, worried about being broke, living paycheck to paycheck **R:** Recovering from emotional insecurity, temporarily unemployed, returning to work

Six Ask for what you need, loans, grants, gifts, inheritance (especially from family) **R:** Not getting help from others, having to pay back loans & debts, bad credit, no $ from family or bank

Seven Hard work leads to good $ and satisfaction **R:** Working hard but frustrated waiting for results, extra expenses coming

Eight Learning a new skill & practicing will lead to good $, apprenticing, creativity, education **R:** Losing interest in school or work, bored (refocus or learn a new skill before $ is lost)

Eight of Pentacles

Nine Making your home a retreat (not a fortress) remodeling, cleaning, new home, gardening. $ is stable & growing **R:** Unexpected home repair or expense, blocking out the world

Ten Money is good or will be soon. Secure and stable home & finances **R:** Major financial loss, may have to sell assets, long term money is good and secure despite this setback

Page News about $ (in the mail or by phone) young person beginning career **R:** Bad news about $, delays in new career

Knight Changing jobs, Person good with money and moving up in the world **R:** Unexpected change in job

Queen Practical, grounded, earthy & friendly **R:** Materialistic, gold digger

King Good business sense, generous, grounded and practical **R:** Greedy, mean, unreliable

Tarot Layouts

Tarot layouts are sometimes called spreads. They bring cohesiveness and understanding to the tarot. While drawing a single card does give us some insight, putting the cards into the context of a layout provides increased understanding. Try one of these layouts with a single card for each position indicated. For more details, you can use two cards staggered for each position as shown to the left.

Quick & Simple Layout

Current situation

Probable Outcome

Suggested Action

Timeline Layout

Distant Past   Past Year   Present   Next 6 Months   Next Year

Keys to Change Layout

What You Hide
from Yourself

Key to Changing
Probable Outcome

Current
Situation

What Led to
the Situation

You in the
Present

Other People
and Influences

Probable
Outcome

Glossary

Athame A ritual knife, usually black handled with a double edged blade.

Bane and Baneful Bane is anything with an undesirable, contrary, or negative influence. It is a very relative term! Something can be baneful to certain people or in certain situations, while being a blessing for others and under different circumstances. Baneful magic is sometimes called *black magic*, however this dichotomy of good/evil – black/white – right/wrong, does not properly apply to magic and Witchcraft as we tend to look beyond overly simplified and limiting binaries.

Book of Shadows (BoS) A combination of journal, scrapbook, spells, rituals, recipes, and correspondences (such as your almanac's Directories). Many Witches keep a BoS, either printed or digitally, and they are very useful for keeping track of experiments and developing your personal path.

Deosil Clockwise movement, also known as sunwise.

Cense & Censing To burn perfume with incense, or to infuse something with incense smoke. Preferred to the culturally appropriated "smudging".

Esbat A ritual held on full moons, sometimes also on new moons.

Manifest and Manifestation Made popular by the book and film *The Secret*, these terms are commonly used in reference to the focusing of one's thoughts upon a desired outcome. Witches have adopted the term as a way to quickly express the focusing of our energy, will, and intent to create change in the physical world or within ourselves. Manifestation can also refer to spiritual forms or entities appearing in the physical world, however in this instance the term *materialization* is better suited.

Sabbat Major festivals, celebrations, and/or holy days celebrated by Witches and many modern Pagans. There are eight Sabbats, the two solstices and two equinoxes (Quarters), and the midpoints in the year between them (Cross-Quarters). The names used for each of the Sabbats, and the number celebrated, vary by tradition.

Syncretic Combining different philosophical, religious, or cultural principles and practices. For example, a Witch might combine Western occultism with ancient folk traditions, neo-Pagan practices, and modern science.

Widdershins Counter-clockwise movement

Words of Power Words of Power are the words used in spells or rituals that are spoken or chanted with a resounding tone to carry your energy out into the universe. Words of Power often rhyme to make them easier to memorize and so they resonate harmoniously. Words of Power are usually repeated to help focus intentions.

Wortcunning is the knowledge of the magical and medicinal properties of herbs, plants, and botanicals, the understanding of how to use these natural materials, and the wisdom of when and why to use botanicals. "Wort" refers to plants, and cunning refers to cleverness and skill.

Author's Note

Thank you for choosing The Practical Witch's Almanac! Through all of life's obligations and challenges, don't forget to celebrate! Enjoy the Sabbats, dance under the full moon, try something new, and have an amazing and magical year!

If you found this almanac helpful, please leave a review on Goodreads. Stay in touch by visiting Practical-Witch.com where you can contact me directly, sync your almanac to the calendar app on your device, and find some extra goodies. Thank you again. I appreciate you. Brightest Blessings to You!

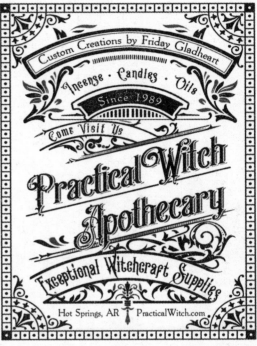

About the Author

Friday Gladheart founded WitchAcademy.org in 1996 where she continues teaching Witchcraft, tarot, and wortcunning. On weekends you'll find her doing tarot readings or performing her "Witcharista" duties inside Arkansas's premier metaphysical shop, *The Parlour* in downtown Hot Springs. Nestled in the back of the shop is Friday's Practical Witch Apothecary. This is a unique old-fashioned, on-demand service where she creates custom magical oils, candles, and incense while you wait. The rest of her time is spent developing her organic teaching garden and Witch Academy campus adjoining a national forest.

Moon Phases of 2022

Times listed are Central Standard Time. Daylight Savings Time is included when in effect March 13-November 6.

New Moon	First Quarter	Full Moon	Third Quarter
Jan 2 12:33 pm	Jan 9 12:11 pm	Jan 17 5:48 pm	Jan 25 7:40 am
Jan 31 11:46 pm	Feb 8 7:50 am	Feb 16 10:56 am	Feb 23 4:32 pm
Mar 2 11:34 am	Mar 10 4:45 am	Mar 18 2:17 am	Mar 25 12:37 am
Apr 1 1:24 am	Apr 9 1:47 am	Apr 16 1:55 pm	Apr 23 6:56 am
Apr 30 3:28 pm	May 8 7:21 pm	May 15 11:14 pm	May 22 1:43 pm
May 30 6:30 am	Jun 7 9:48 am	**Jun 14** 6:51 am	Jun 20 10:10 pm
Jun 28 9:52 pm	Jul 6 9:14 pm	**Jul 13** 1:37 pm	Jul 20 9:18 am
Jul 28 12:54 pm	Aug 5 6:06 am	Aug 11 8:35 pm	Aug 18 11:36 pm
Aug 27 3:17 am	Sep 3 1:07 pm	Sep 10 4:59 am	Sep 17 4:52 pm
Sep 25 4:54 pm	Oct 2 7:14 pm	Oct 9 3:54 pm	Oct 17 12:15 pm
Oct 25 5:48 am	Nov 1 1:37 am	Nov 8 5:02 am	Nov 16 7:27 am
Nov 23 4:57 pm	Nov 30 8:36 am	Dec 7 10:08 pm	Dec 16 2:56 am
Dec 23 4:16 am	Dec 29 7:20 pm		

*Supermoon dates are in **bold**.*

SUBSCRIBE!

For as little as $15/month, you can

support a small, independent publisher

and get every book that we publish—

delivered to your doorstep!

www.**Microcosm.Pub/BFF**

BE THE PERSON YOU WANT TO BE AND CHANGE THE WORLD AROUND YOU AT MICROCOSM.PUB

PREVIOUS ALMANACS ALSO CONTAIN INFORMATION THAT IS ETERNALLY RELEVANT AND TOPICAL